BACKPACK

Second Edition

Mario Herrera · Diane Pinkley

PEARSON
Longman

Contents

Backpack Song

It's time to open Backpack
and see what we can see.
We'll have lots of adventures.
Explore Backpack with me!

Backpack is full of fun things
we use each day in school.
Stories, puzzles, songs, and games—
Backpack is really cool!

It's time to open Backpack
and see what we can see.
We'll have lots of adventures.
Explore Backpack with me!

Backpack is full of fun and facts,
projects and pictures, too.
We're learning English, we're never bored.
There are great new things to do!

It's time to open Backpack
and see what we can see.
We'll have lots of adventures.
Explore Backpack with me!

1 From Morning to Night

TRACK A3

1 Read. Listen and sing.

Exactly Ed

Every day at exactly 6:45,
  Ed gets out of bed.
Not 6:44, or 6:46,
  because he's Exactly Ed.

Every day at exactly 7:00,
  Ed gets ready to go.
He washes his face, combs his hair,
  and gets dressed—
  never fast and never slow.

He does the same things
  at the same time every day.
Because he's Exactly Ed,
  it just has to be that way.

Every day at exactly 7:15,
  Ed eats his breakfast.
Then he brushes his teeth,
  and he walks to school.
So at 8:00 he sits at his desk.

(Chorus)

TRACK A4

2 Listen. Point and say.

TRACK A5

3 Listen and stick.

TRACK A7

4 Listen. Look and read.

Before school

1. She takes a shower at 7:00 in the morning.

2. He gets dressed at 7:25 in the morning.

3. She eats breakfast at 7:30 in the morning.

4. He feeds his bird at 7:45 in the morning.

Reading: social studies; vocabulary and grammar in context

After school

5. She does her homework at 3:30 in the afternoon.

6. She plays video games at 4:15 in the afternoon.

7. She has a tae-kwon-do lesson at 5:10 in the afternoon.

8. He watches cartoons on TV at 5:30 in the afternoon.

TRACK A8

5 Point. Ask and answer.

TRACK A9

6 Point. Ask and answer.

Question formation; *do/does*; routine actions

Grammar

What does	he / she	do **before** school?	He / She	eats breakfast **before** school.
What do you do **after** school?			I watch TV **after** school.	

7 Look at the clocks. Read. Write *before* or *after*.

David

Sun-mi

Tim

1. David brushes his teeth ___after___ he eats breakfast.
2. Sun-mi watches TV ______________ she does her homework.
3. Tim gets dressed ______________ he combs his hair.
4. David eats breakfast ______________ he brushes his teeth.
5. Sun-mi does her homework ______________ she watches TV.
6. Tim combs his hair ______________ he gets dressed.

8 Read and circle.

Hi! I'm David, and my brother's name is Tim. I get up at 6:45. Tim gets up at 7:00. I take a shower at 7:10, but Tim doesn't. He takes a shower at 7:25. I play soccer at 4:30. Tim plays soccer at 4:45. I do my homework at 6:30, but Tim doesn't. He does his homework at 8:00.

1. David gets up before Tim.	(yes)	no
2. Tim takes a shower before David.	yes	no
3. David plays soccer after Tim.	yes	no
4. Tim does his homework after David.	yes	no

Questions with *do/does*; simple present; *before/after*

9 Look and write.

1. She watches TV after school.

2. He ______________ after school.

3. I ______________ before school.

4. She ______________ after school.

5. He ______________ before school.

10 Ask three friends. Tell the class.

Name	After School	Time
Katia	rides her bike	3:30
1.		
2.		
3.		

Routine actions; *before/after*; questions with *do*; time

11 Listen. Write the letter.

1. e
2. ____
3. ____
4. ____
5. ____

a

b

c

d

e

12 Listen. Read and chant.

After School

I work hard in school all day,
so after school it's time to play.
I go and get my ball and bat,
and my favorite baseball hat.
I meet my friends at five o'clock sharp,
and then play baseball 'til it's dark.
I go back home to watch TV,
and then eat dinner with my family.
I do my homework and help my mom,
and then it's nine—the day is gone.
So as I go to bed I say,
tomorrow is another day!

See Sound and Spelling Handbook p. 110

Betty Backwards reads her mom a story.
She reads from the end to the beginning.
She goes to sleep after her mom does.

(Betty does everything backwards.
She isn't like you and me.
Betty does things differently!)

Betty Backwards

by Diane Pinkley

Betty Backwards gets up at ten o'clock at night. She eats dinner after she brushes her teeth. She gets dressed in her pajamas before she goes out to play.

(Betty does everything backwards.
She isn't like you and me.
Betty does things differently!)

TRACK A13

Betty Backwards goes to school on weekends.
She plays soccer before she goes to school.
She walks her cat after school.

(Betty does everything backwards.
She isn't like you and me.
Betty does things differently!)

Betty Backwards has breakfast before she goes to bed. She eats her dessert before her vegetables. She gets dressed in a skirt and blouse before she goes to sleep.

(Betty does everything backwards. She isn't like you and me. Betty does things differently!)

Twist and Talk

Art Project

Cut out the paper strips on page 127.
Make a talking tube.

Content connection: art; language arts

Values

Celebrate Special Days

Look and read. Talk.

What special days do you celebrate? What do you do on special days? Talk and write.

Know It? Show It!

Spin. Ask and answer.

What does she do before school?

She eats breakfast.

Ask people what time it is.

Excuse me.
What time is it, please?

It's 4:50, ma'am.

Thank you.

Performance assessment
See Assessment Package pp. 87–89, 93, 101, and 110–111.

2 Helping Hands

1 Read. Listen and sing. TRACK A14

Helpers

There are many helping hands
in my family.
We like to help each other out
in our community.

Firefighters keep us safe—
police officers, too.
My uncle John's a firefighter.
What does your uncle do?

Farmers help to keep us fed—
chefs and waiters, too.
My father is a farmer.
What does your father do?

(Chorus)

Teachers help us learn a lot—
TV reporters, too.
My mother is a teacher.
What does your mother do?

(Chorus)

Helping occupations; family members

TRACK A15

2 Listen. Point and say.

1. My sister is a secretary.
   She types letters.
2. My grandfather is a barber.
   He cuts hair.
3. My aunt is a mail carrier.
   She brings the mail.
4. My father is a coach.
   He teaches soccer.
5. My cousin is a salesperson.
   She sells clothes.
6. My brother is a waiter.
   He serves food.

1

2

3

4

5

6

TRACK A16

3 Listen. Stick and say.

What does your sister do?

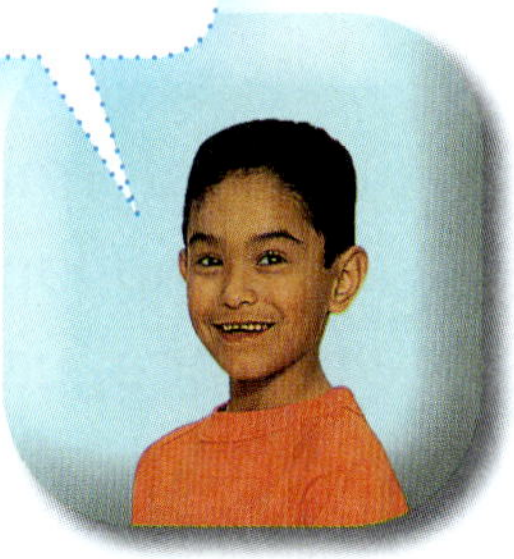

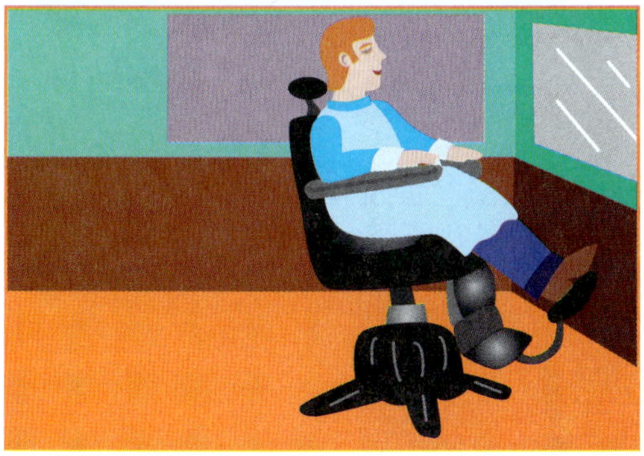

Language in the Real World

TRACK A18

4 Listen. Look and read.

Health Workers

Health workers help us stay healthy. Dentists fix our teeth. Doctors help sick people get well. Nurses give shots. Exercise instructors help us use our muscles. Vets help sick animals.

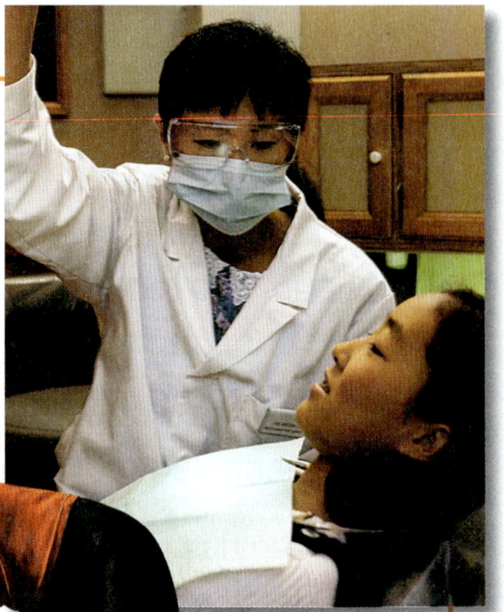

Information Workers

Information workers help us get information. Teachers help us learn math, science, and English. TV reporters tell us what is happening in the world. Journalists write stories for newspapers. Computer programmers help us get information fast.

Reading: social studies; vocabulary and grammar in context

Construction Workers

Construction workers help us live in comfort. Plumbers give us running hot and cold water. Electricians put in electricity for lights, heat, and TV sets. Architects design buildings. Carpenters build things out of wood.

TRACK A19

5 Point. Ask and answer.

TRACK A20

6 Ask and answer.

Question formation; contractions; occupations

Grammar

What does he / she do?		He / She	**is** an architect.
What do they do?		They**'re** architects.	

7 Look and write.

1. What does she do? She's a police officer.
2. What do they do? They're ______________________
3. What does he do? He's a ______________________
4. What do they do? They're ______________________

8 Read and write.

Hi! My name is Eric. My family likes to help other people. My father helps students learn math and science. My mother helps sick animals get well. My uncle builds things out of wood for people to use. My aunt helps people exercise to stay healthy. I want to help people, too. I want to design buildings for my community.

1. Eric's father is a ______________________
2. Eric's mother is a ______________________
3. Eric's uncle is a ______________________
4. Eric's aunt is an ______________________
5. Eric wants to be an ______________________

Grammar

What do dentists do? They **fix our teeth**.

9 Look and write.

1 

2 

3 

4 

5 

6 

1. Architects design buildings.
2. __________
3. __________
4. __________
5. __________
6. __________

bring mail
build things out of wood
design buildings
get information
serve food
teach sports

10 Ask a friend. Tell the class.

(Me) __________

(My friend) __________

TRACK A22

11 Listen. Write T for *true* and F for *false*.

1. a. T
   b. ____
2. a. ____
   b. ____
3. a. ____
   b. ____
4. a. ____
   b. ____

TRACK A23

12 Listen. Read and chant.

One Day

One day I'll be all grown up
and ready for a job.
Maybe I'll be a TV reporter
like my uncle Bob.
Or maybe I'll be a soccer star
and sign my name for fans.
Or maybe I'll be a singer
in a famous band.
Or maybe I'll be an astronaut
and fly in outer space.
Or maybe I'll be a doctor
like my cousin Grace.

See Sound and Spelling Handbook p. 111

Listening for main idea and details; stress, rhythm, and intonation

My uncle is a clown. He makes people laugh.

My aunt is a juggler.
She can keep many things
in the air at the same time.

Being a circus family is hard
work—and fun.

A Circus Family

by Diallo Lawton

Hi. I'm Natasha, and I work with my
family in the circus.

We all work very hard, but every day
in the circus world is exciting!

TRACK A24

My grandfather is an electrician.
He controls all the special lights for the circus.

My grandmother is a tailor.
She sews beautiful costumes for people to wear.

My father is a trapeze artist.
He swings on a trapeze and flies through the air.

My mother is an acrobat. She can turn cartwheels and jump very high.

Family Tree

Cut out the frames from page 129.
Make a family tree.

Values

Help Others

Look and read. Talk.

John is opening the door for his grandmother.

Emily is giving her seat to a mother and her baby.

Carl is putting the game back for his friends. Sarah is putting the book back for her friends.

What about you? How do you help others? Talk and write.

Know It? Show It!

Write four words from the list. Listen. Make an X. When you have all Xs, say *Bingo*.

journalist	________	________
________	☆	electrician
TV reporter	mail carrier	________

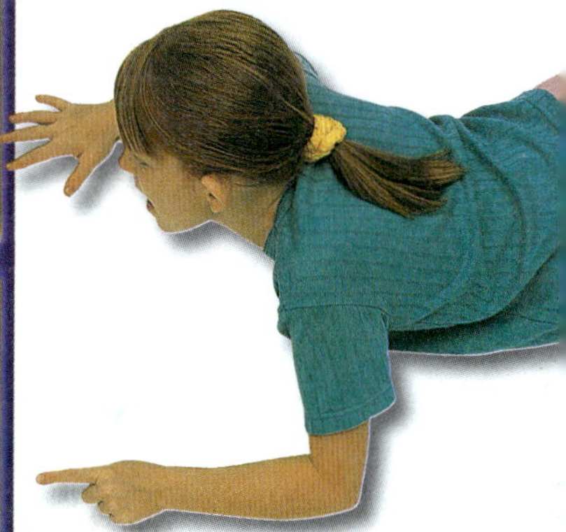

- architect
- coach
- dentist
- plumber
- secretary
- teacher
- waiter

Draw what you want to be.

Unit 2
☆
I can do it!

Performance assessment
See Assessment Package pp. 87–89, 92, 102, and 110–111.

3 Pen Pals

TRACK A25

1 Read. Listen and sing.

Friends

Some of my friends live nearby,
and some live far away—
in France, Japan, and Paraguay.
I don't see them day to day.

We send each other e-mails,
photos, and birthday cards.
I love to hear from all my friends.
It's fun and it isn't hard.

Friends with smiling faces,
pen pals in distant places.
I've got friends I write to
near and far.

I write about my city life
and what I see each day—
the crowded streets, the noisy cars,
and parks where children play.

One pen pal lives in the country.
He writes me about the farm.
He feeds chickens in the yard
and milks cows in the barn.

(Chorus)

2 Listen. Point and say.

TRACK A26

There is noise and excitement in the city. There are many people and cars on the streets. There are lots of stores, movie theaters with bright lights, tall buildings, and restaurants. There are parks, museums, and libraries.

There is peace and quiet in the country. There are big barns and houses with fences. There are lots of trees, flowers, and crops in the fields. There are ponds and lakes for fishing and swimming. There are many animals.

3 Listen. Stick and say.

TRACK A27

City and country life; *there is/there are*

TRACK A29

4 Listen. Look and read.

This is a picture of my pen pal. He lives on a farm in the country. Every morning he has to go to the barn to collect the eggs and feed the chickens. He sometimes milks the cow.

After school, he usually helps his father with the chores. Sometimes he and his father have to clean the barn or paint the fence. He goes to bed early because he has to get up at 6:00 A.M.

Reading: social studies; vocabulary and grammar in context

This is my pen pal. She lives in the city. She lives in an apartment in a tall building.

Every morning, she has to make her bed and feed her cat. She never walks to school. She always takes the school bus.

After school, she usually waits for her brother. They have to take another bus to go to their music lessons. My pen pal loves music.

TRACK A30

5 Point. Ask and answer.

What does he have to do?

He has to collect the eggs.

TRACK A31

6 Ask and answer.

What does he sometimes do?

He sometimes milks the cow.

Question formation; adverbs of frequency; chores

Grammar

What **does**	he she	**have to** do?	He She	**has to** feed the cat.
What **do**	you they	**have to** do?	I They	**have to** feed the cat.

7 Write *has to* or *have to*.

1. What does he have to do? He ______________ go to bed at 8:30.
2. What do they have to do? They ______________ paint the fence.
3. What does she have to do? She ______________ take the bus.
4. What do they have to do? They ______________ practice the piano.

8 Read and write.

Hi! My name is Monica. Today is a busy day. First, I have to clean my room and feed my bird. Then I have to go to the library with my mother. We have to return some books. Then we are going shopping. After that, I have to practice the piano. After dinner, I'm going to write a letter to my pen pal.

1. What are three things Monica has to do?

____

____

____

2. What do Monica and her mother have to do?

____

____

What questions with *do/does*;
have/has to + verb

9 Ask four friends. Tell the class.

clean my room	go to soccer practice
do my homework	make my bed
feed my bird	practice the piano
go shopping	write to my pen pal

What do you have to do today?

I have to make my bed and feed my cat.

Name	I have to . . .	
Mounira	make my bed	feed my cat
1.		
2.		
3.		
4.		

10 Talk about what you do.

Do you make your bed?

Sometimes.

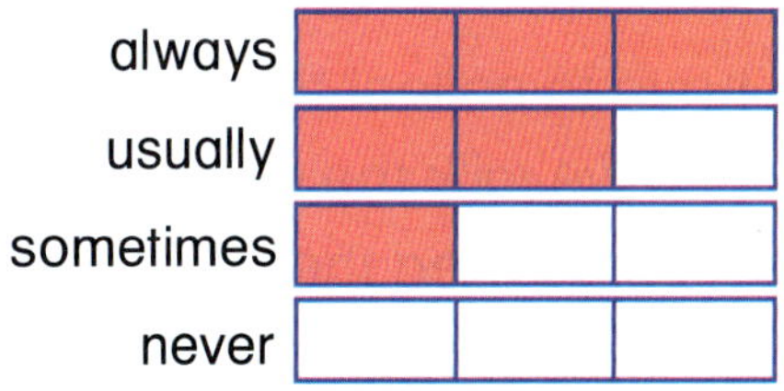

TRACK A33

11 Listen. Write the letter.

1. ____
2. ____
3. ____
4. ____
5. ____

a

b

c

d

e

TRACK A34

12 Listen. Read and chant.

A Country Visit

Pen pal, I'm so happy
you're coming to stay with me.
You can help me with my chores.
I have lots of work, you see.

First, we have to collect the eggs,
and then we milk the cow.
Next, we have to feed the chickens.
I'll be glad to show you how.

But after work, we'll rest and play.
I promise you'll love your country stay!
And when I visit your home, too,
I'll help you with all you have to do!

Listening for details; stress, rhythm, and intonation

See Sound and Spelling Handbook p. 112

A City Visit

Hi! I'm Terry from Australia.
I live on a farm in the country.
Today I'm flying to Tokyo, Japan.
My pen pal Masahiro is waiting
at the airport!

TRACK A35

One of my favorite places in Tokyo is Ueno Park.
There are lots of trees and gardens.
There is a wonderful zoo in the park, too.
Tokyo is a great city to visit!

I am staying with Masahiro and his family.
They live in the Ikebukuro district of Tokyo.
They have an apartment on the third floor of a tall building.
Sometimes we run up and down all the stairs.

There are lots of interesting buildings, stores, and restaurants in Tokyo.
There are many people and cars on the streets.
Tokyo is an exciting and busy city.
There is always something fun to do.

City or Country

Cut out the pictures on page 131.
Make a city or country scene.

Content connection: social studies; art

Values

Do Your Chores

Look and read. Talk.

What chores do you have to do? Talk and write.

Know It? Show It!

Spin. Ask and answer.

What does he have to do?

He has to feed the chickens.

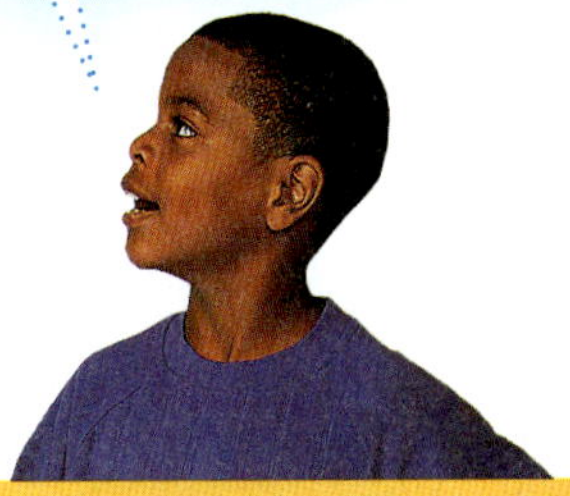

Make a book.

He usually collects eggs before school.

Performance assessment
See Assessment Package pp. 87–89, 94, 103, 110–111 and 112–113.

4 Amazing Animals

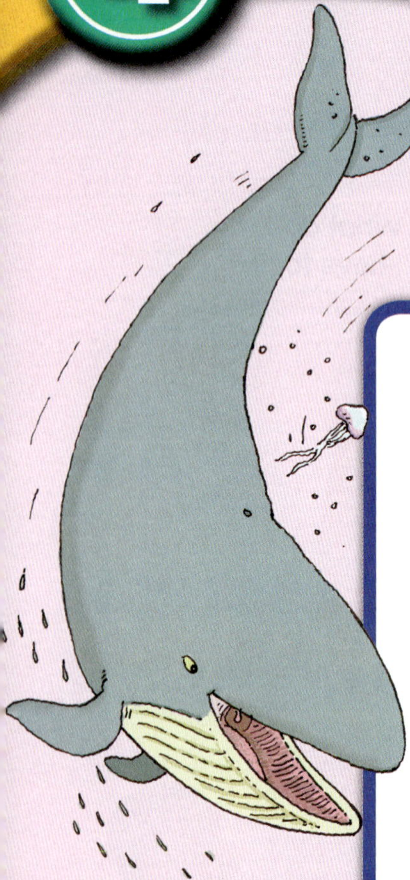

TRACK A36

1 Read. Listen and sing.

Animals

Some of the animals live in the sea.
Whales swim under water,
much faster than you and me.

Some of the animals fly in the air—
bats, eagles, all kinds of birds.
How did they get there?

Animals live in all kinds of places
with all kinds of weather.
Animals have all kinds of faces
with horns and teeth and feathers.

Some of the animals live in ice and snow—
polar bears and penguins.
They like it really cold.

Some of the animals live in desert sand.
Ducks, parrots, and fish can't,
but lizards and camels can.

(Chorus)

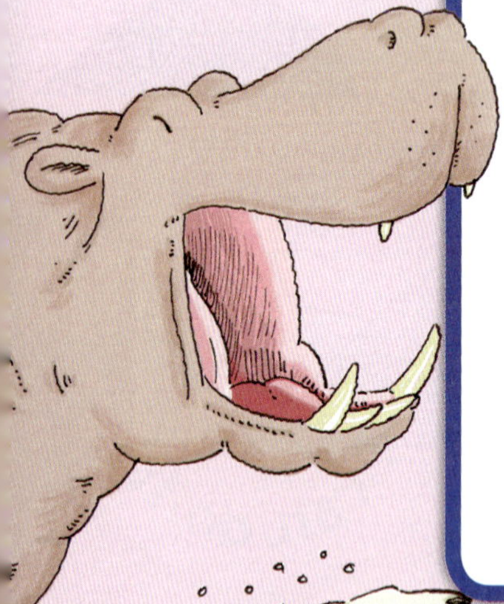

TRACK A37

2 Listen. Point and say.

Animals live in many different places.

1. A deer lives in the forest.
2. A penguin lives in the ice and snow.
3. A camel lives in the desert.
4. An ostrich lives on the plains.
5. A parrot lives in the rain forest.
6. A whale lives in the ocean.

3 Stick and say.

Language in the Real World

TRACK A39

4 Listen. Look and read.

Most sharks in the ocean can't stop moving; if they do, they can't breathe. Sharks grow new teeth every eight days. Some sharks can have as many as 30,000 teeth in their lifetime!

Egyptian plovers can live in the mouths of crocodiles! They clean the crocodiles' teeth. Crocodiles never eat this bird!

Giraffes live on the plains. They are very tall, and so they can reach high into trees to eat the leaves. Male giraffes fight with their horns and necks. Giraffes can clean their own ears with their 21-inch (53-cm) tongues!

Camels live in the desert. They can go without food or water for a long time. They can live off the fat in their humps. Camels can't sweat, so they don't lose water from their bodies.

Octopuses like the warm parts of the ocean. Some octopuses can squeeze fish with their long tentacles, and some of them kill with a poison bite. Octopuses can change colors any time they want, and they can squirt black ink when they want to hide from an enemy!

Kangaroos live on the plains. They have strong legs and can jump as high as 9 feet (2.7 m). Kangaroos can run 40 miles (64 km) an hour, but they can't walk backwards! They can go without water for a very long time. Female kangaroos keep their babies in their pouches.

TRACK A40

5 Point. Ask and answer.

Where do sharks live?

In the ocean.

TRACK A41

6 Ask and answer.

What can sharks do?

They can grow new teeth.

Question formation; *can*

Grammar

	you		I		I	
	he		He		He	
What **can**	she	do?	She	**can** run fast.	She	**can't** fly.
	it		It		It	
	they		They		They	

7 Look and write. Use *can* or *can't*.

fly

jump

walk

climb

1. What can they do? They ______________________
2. What can it do? It ______________________
3. What can't it do? It ______________________
4. What can you do? I ______________________

8 Read and write. Use *can* or *can't*.

python

There are over 3,000 types of snakes in the world. Snakes can live underground, in trees, or in the ocean. Some snakes, such as pythons, can grow to be very long. A python can squeeze an antelope and then eat it whole, little by little. Some snakes are very small, the size of a pencil. Snakes can't walk or run because they don't have legs. They can't close their eyes because they don't have eyelids.

1. Snakes ______________ live in different places.
2. A python ______________ grow to be very long.
3. A python ______________ eat a whole antelope.
4. Snakes ______________ walk or run.
5. Snakes ______________ close their eyes.

antelope

Questions with *what*; *can/can't* + verb; subject pronouns

9 Ask and answer.

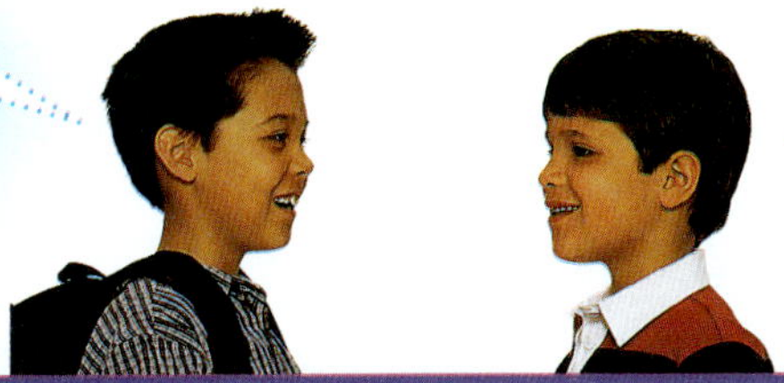

An animal that . . .	Animal
lives in ice and snow and can't fly	a penguin
1. can go without water for a long time	
2. can change its color	
3. can squeeze other animals	
4. can reach high into trees to eat leaves	
5. can hold a bird in its mouth	
6. keeps its babies in a pouch	

10 A. What can you do? Write.

____

____

____

____

____

B. Tell a group what you can do.

TRACK A43

11 Listen. Write the number.

TRACK A44

12 Listen. Read and chant.

If I Could Be an Animal

If I could be an animal, a shark is what I'd be.
I'd grow new teeth and skip the dentist.
That sounds great to me.

If I could be an animal, a penguin is what I'd be.
Formally dressed, I'd play in the snow.
That sounds fun to me.

If I could be an animal, a python is what I'd be.
I'd squeeze my dinner and eat for a week.
That sounds good to me.

If I could be an animal, a giraffe is what I'd be.
I'd clean my ears without taking a bath.
That sounds cool to me.

See Sound and Spelling Handbook p. 113

Listening for main idea and details; stress, rhythm, and intonation

Snake's Flying Lesson

Based on a Mexican Folktale

Retold by Diane Pinkley

One day Snake is talking to two birds.

"I live in the desert on the hot ground. I can't fly," says Snake.

"Everybody knows snakes can't fly," say the birds.

"I want to fly like you! Help me!" says Snake.

"We can try," say the birds.

TRACK A45

Snake opens his mouth to bite Eagle.

He falls through the air down to the ground.

He lands on a cactus. Ouch!

"Hold on tight, friend. Don't open your mouth or you'll fall!" say the birds.

The birds carry Snake high in the air.

The air is cool. The sun shines through the white clouds.

Flying is wonderful! thinks Snake.

"Well, well. A silly snake who thinks it can fly!" says Eagle. "Are those feathers down there on your tail? Can you fly without that stick in your mouth?"

Snake gets very angry.

Animal Mobiles

Cut out the shapes and words on page 133. Make an animal mobile to talk about.

Giraffes and ostriches live on the plains. Zebras live on the plains, too.

Content connection: science; social studies

Help Protect Animals

What can you do? Look and read. Talk.

Go to the library. Find and read books about threatened and endangered animals. Watch TV shows. Talk to vets and other people who help animals.

Decide how your group can help protect animals. Will you write letters? Will you make posters?

Write about what you and people in your community can do to help.

Know It? Show It!

Look at the picture. Write the name of the animal.

Make an animal mask. Talk about your animal.

I'm a tiger. I live in the forest. I can run fast.

Performance assessment
See Assessment Package pp. 87–89, 95, 104, and 110–111.

5 Rain or Shine

TRACK A46

1 Read. Listen and sing.

Playing Outside

Hey, where's my sweater?
It's a cool and windy day.
I need a cap and sweater
to go outside and play.

Hey, where's my winter coat?
It's a cold and snowy day.
I need a coat, hat, and gloves
to go outside and play.

When the seasons change,
the clothes I wear change, too.
No matter what the weather is,
I play outside—don't you?

Hey, where's my raincoat?
It's a wet and rainy day.
I need a raincoat and some boots
to go outside and play.

Hey, where's my swimsuit?
It's a hot and sunny day.
I need my suit and sandals
to go outside and play.

(Chorus—repeat)

2 Listen. Point and say.

TRACK A47

1. Today it's rainy. Puddles are everywhere!
2. Yesterday it was sunny.
3. Tuesday it was snowy. Snowflakes were everywhere!
4. Wednesday it was cloudy.
5. Monday it was windy. Leaves were everywhere!

3 Stick and say.

today

Weather; simple present and past (*be*); *yesterday/today*; days of the week

TRACK A49

4 Listen. Look and read.

Weather is different in different places. Weather changes with the seasons.

Montreal, Canada

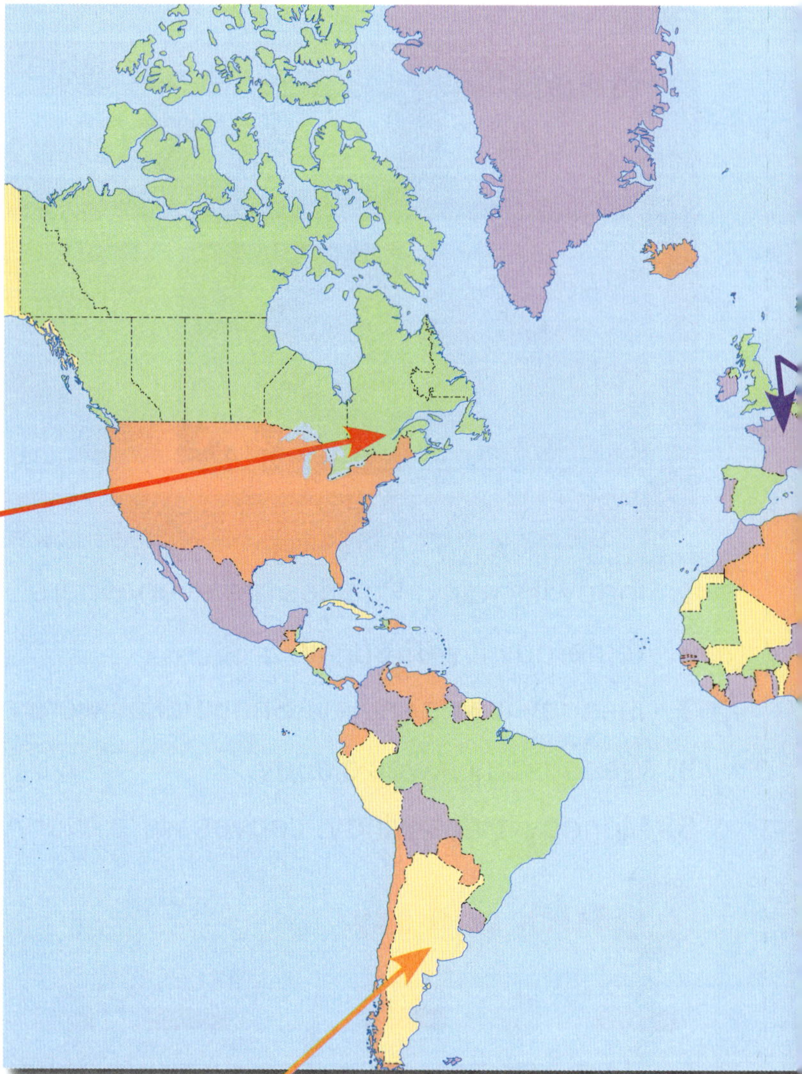

Marie lives in Montreal, Canada. In winter, when it is cold and snowy, she wears a hat, a scarf, and a warm coat. She also wears gloves and boots.

Buenos Aires, Argentina

Angela lives in Buenos Aires, Argentina. When it is winter in Canada, it is summer in Argentina. Angela wears a T-shirt, shorts, and sandals when it is hot and sunny.

Reading: science; social studies; vocabulary and grammar in context

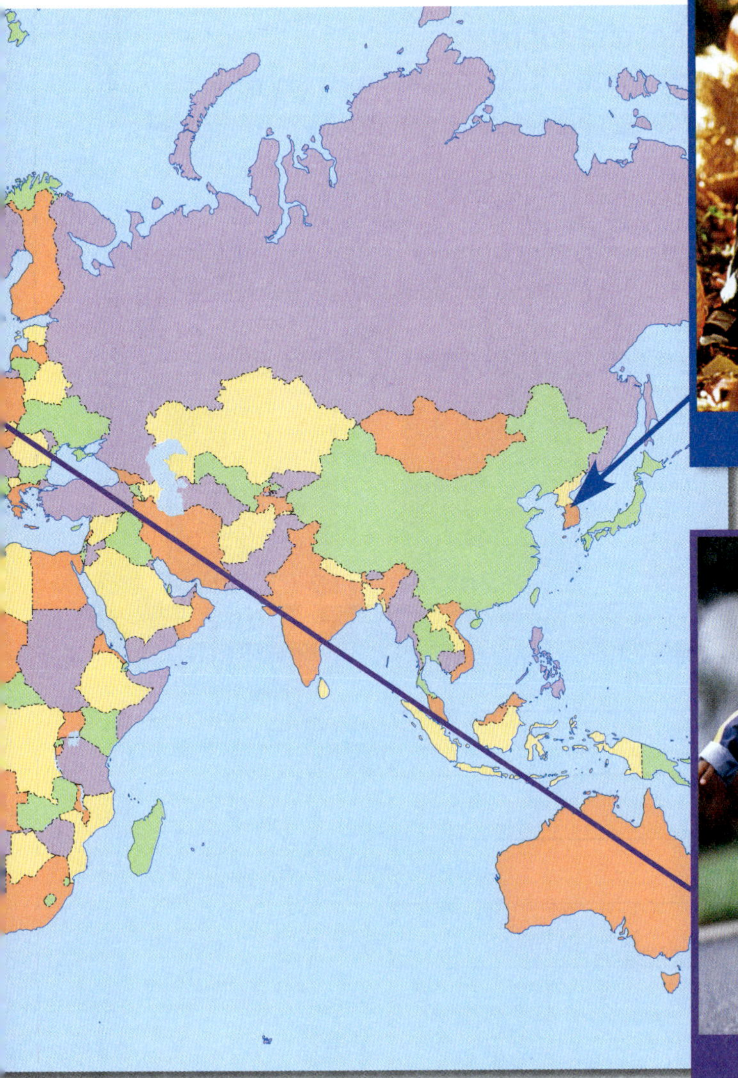

Seoul, Korea

Kwan-su lives in Seoul, Korea. In fall, when it is cool and windy, he wears a jacket or sweater, shirt, and jeans. He wears socks and sneakers, too.

Paris, France

Pierre lives in Paris, France. In spring, when it is rainy, he wears a raincoat and boots. He carries an umbrella, too. (He loves to play in puddles!)

TRACK A50

5 Point. Ask and answer.

TRACK A51

6 Point. Ask and answer.

Question formation; weather and seasons

Grammar

What **is** the weather like today?	It**'s** hot and sunny.
What **was** the weather like yesterday?	It **was** windy. Leaves **were** everywhere!

7 Write *is* or *was* and a weather word.

1. Wednesday it ______________________________
2. Friday it ______________________________
3. Today it ______________________________
4. Thursday it ______________________________
5. Tuesday it ______________________________

8 Read and write.

And now let's talk about the weather. The weather was crazy the first part of the week. Sunday it was sunny. Monday it was cloudy. Tuesday it was rainy. Wednesday it was windy. And today? Well, this morning it was sunny. At 12:30, it was cloudy. And now, this afternoon, it's raining! Wear a raincoat and boots, and take an umbrella when you go outside!

1. What was the weather like on Wednesday?

____

2. What was the weather like this morning?

____

3. What is the weather like this afternoon?

____

9 Ask four friends. Tell the class.

What do you like to wear on weekends?

I like to wear my shorts, a T-shirt, and sandals.

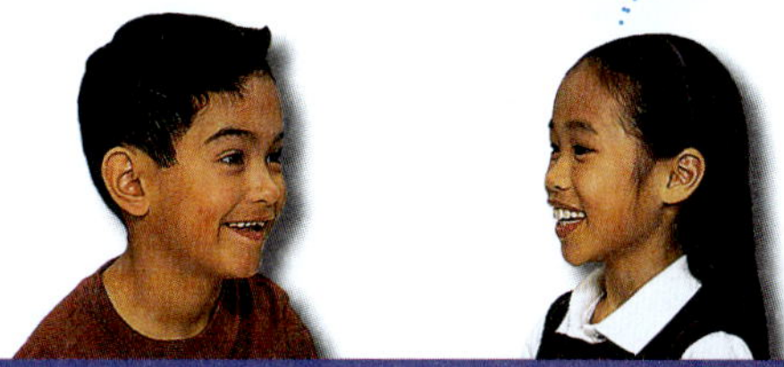

Name	Likes to wear . . .
Sylvia	shorts sandals T-shirt
1.	
2.	
3.	
4.	

10 Make riddles. Ask and answer.

People wear coats, hats, and gloves. What season is it?

It's winter.

TRACK A53

11 Listen and write.

1. It's ____________________
2. It's ____________________
3. ____________________
4. ____________________
5. It's ____________________

TRACK A54

12 Listen. Read and chant.

Favorite Seasons

Winter's my favorite season.
It's the best of all.
I play in the snow or slide on my sled.
In winter, I have a ball!

Spring is my favorite season.
It's the best of all.
I plant new flowers or play in the park.
In spring, I have a ball!

Summer's my favorite season.
It's the best of all.
I go on a picnic or swim in the lake.
In summer, I have a ball!

Fall is my favorite season.
It's the best of all.
I jump in the leaves or ride my bike.
In fall, I have a ball!

See Sound and Spelling Handbook p. 114

Listening for main idea and details; stress, rhythm, and intonation

"Oh! A coat!"

"That was your grandfather's coat when he was a boy," says Palluq. "Now you are big. Now you can wear it."

Meekitjuk is very happy.

"With this warm coat," he says, "I can go out in the ice and snow!"

A New Old Coat

by Diane Pinkley

Meekitjuk, an Inuit boy, lives with his mother, Palluq.

"Winter is coming," says Meekitjuk.

"Yes. The weather is changing," says Palluq, "and here we are at our winter house."

TRACK A55

"Mother!" says Meekitjuk. "Look!"

"What is it?" asks Palluq.

"My winter coat is too small," says Meekitjuk. "How can I go out in the ice and snow?"

"It is cold and snowy for many months. You need a new coat. I can make a coat from this bag," says Palluq. "Empty the bag."

Meekitjuk isn't happy.

I don't want a coat made from an ugly old bag! he thinks.

Four Seasons Poster

Cut out the pictures on page 135.
Make a poster.

Science Project

In summer, I wear shorts and a T-shirt. I wear a swimsuit, too. I like to swim in the lake.

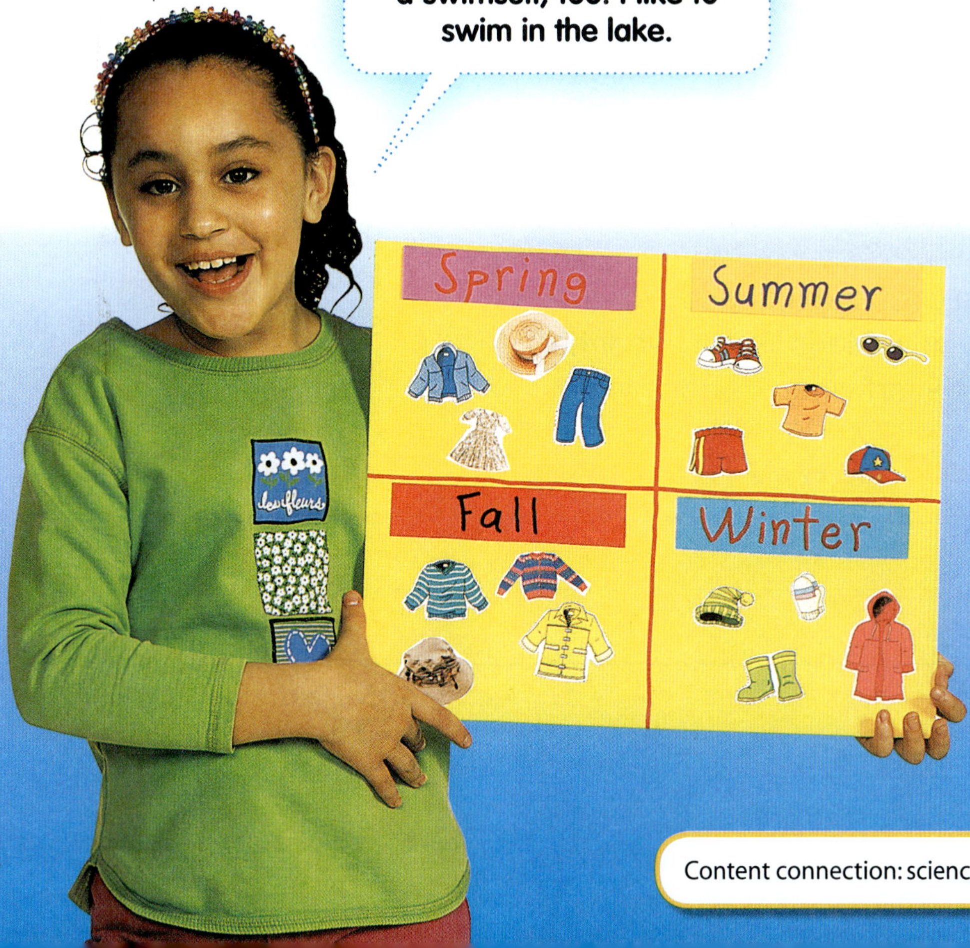

Values

Be Prepared!

Look and read. Talk.

She carries an umbrella when it's cloudy. Tania wears a raincoat and boots when it's rainy.

She has a warm coat and hat ready for a cold and snowy day. Maria likes to wear her red gloves and a scarf when it's cold, too.

He wears sunscreen and a hat when he's going out in the sun. Paul always has his swimsuit ready when it is hot and sunny.

What about you? How are you prepared? Talk and write.

Know It? Show It!

Take turns shopping for and selling clothes.

Make a weather chart.

Performance assessment
See Assessment Package pp. 87–89, 96, 105, and 110–111.

6 Our Five Senses

1 Read. Listen and sing. TRACK A56

Street Fair

At the street fair I can see
so many things to buy—
jewelry, clothes, toys, and pets,
and books piled up high.

At the street fair I can smell
delicious food to eat.
I can taste the popcorn
and the ice-cream cones so sweet.

At the street fair, at the street fair—
my senses come alive.
At the street fair, at the street fair—
one, two, three, four, five.

At the street fair I can hear
laughter from the crowd.
A little monkey with a drum
and sticks is playing loud.

At the street fair I can look at
things both old and new.
I love to look and touch them all,
then buy just one or two.

(Chorus)

TRACK A57

2 Listen. Point and say. Write.

Our bodies tell us about the world.

1. We see with our eyes.
2. We hear with our ears.
3. We smell with our nose.
4. We taste with our tongue.
5. We touch with our fingers.

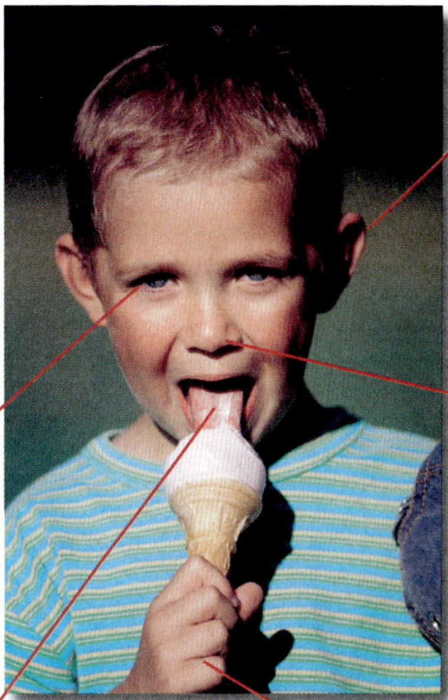

______________ ______________ ______________ ______________ ______________

3 Stick and say.

1.

2.

3.

4.

5.

TRACK A59

4 **Listen. Look and read.**

Our five senses—hearing, smell, taste, touch, and sight—tell us about the world.

Hearing

We use our ears to hear. A trumpet sounds loud. Rain sounds soft. Wind chimes sound pretty. A fire truck siren sounds *very* loud.

Smell

We use our nose to smell. Flowers and perfume smell sweet. Soap smells fresh and clean. Paint smells strong. Food smells delicious.

Taste

We use our tongue to taste. Candy tastes sweet. A lemon tastes sour. Corn chips taste salty. Salsa tastes spicy. Most food tastes delicious, but some medicine tastes bad!

Reading: science; vocabulary and grammar in context

Touch

We use our fingers to touch. Glass feels smooth. A pin feels sharp. Sandpaper feels rough. A rabbit's fur feels soft. A desk feels hard. Glue feels sticky.

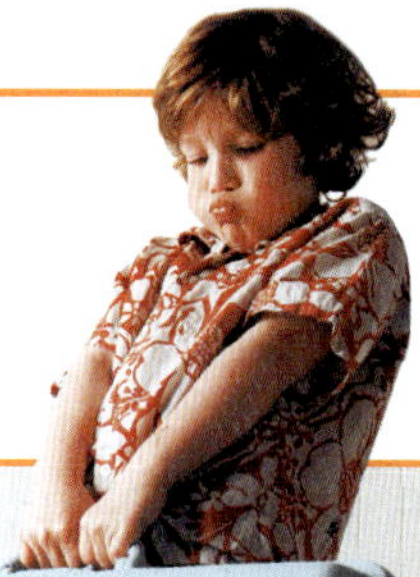

Sight

We use our eyes to see. The suitcase looks heavy. The dog looks sad. Flowers look beautiful. Babies look happy. Soccer players look hot and tired.

TRACK A60

5 Point. Ask and answer.

TRACK A61

6 Point. Describe.

Grammar

How **does** the ice cream **taste**?	It **tastes** sweet.
How **do** the wind chimes **sound**?	They **sound** pretty.

7 Look and write. Use *happy, loud, salty,* and *sharp.*

1. How does popcorn taste? It ________________
2. How does a pin feel? It ________________
3. How do drums sound? They ________________
4. How does the baby look? He ________________

8 Read and write.

Yesterday was a wonderful day. I went to a street fair. There were so many things to see and do! There was a good band. The music was loud. The pizza was good. The hamburgers were delicious. There was a man with comic books for sale. There was a woman with a kitten for sale. It was so cute, and its fur was so soft! It was a great day.

1. How was yesterday?

____

2. How was the music?

____

3. How were the hamburgers?

____

4. Describe the kitten.

____

9 Ask five friends. Tell the class.

Why do you like pizza?

Because it tastes great!

feel look smell sound taste

Name	Why do you like . . .	Because . . .
Marta		it tastes great
1.		
2.		
3.		
4.		
5.		

10 Look around your classroom. Write.

1. Find something sharp. pencil ____________________
2. Find something hard. ____________________
3. Find something sweet. ____________________
4. Find something smooth. ____________________
5. Find something heavy. ____________________

Questions with *why*; *because*; verbs of sensation

TRACK A63

11 Listen. Write the number.

TRACK A64

12 Listen. Read and chant.

More!

Sister, Sister, give me more.
This candy tastes so sweet.
If you love me, give me more.
This candy is a treat!

Mama, Mama, give me more.
That pizza smells so good.
If you love me, give me more.
Thanks. I knew you would!

Daddy, Daddy, give me more.
My piggy bank feels so light.
If you love me, give me more.
More coins will make it right!

Listening for details; stress, rhythm, and intonation

See Sound and Spelling Handbook p. 115

Dora goes into the other room.

She sees a beautiful parrot.

"The feathers feel so soft!" she says.

"Her name is Polly," says Dora's mom.

Dora the Detective

by Mario Herrera

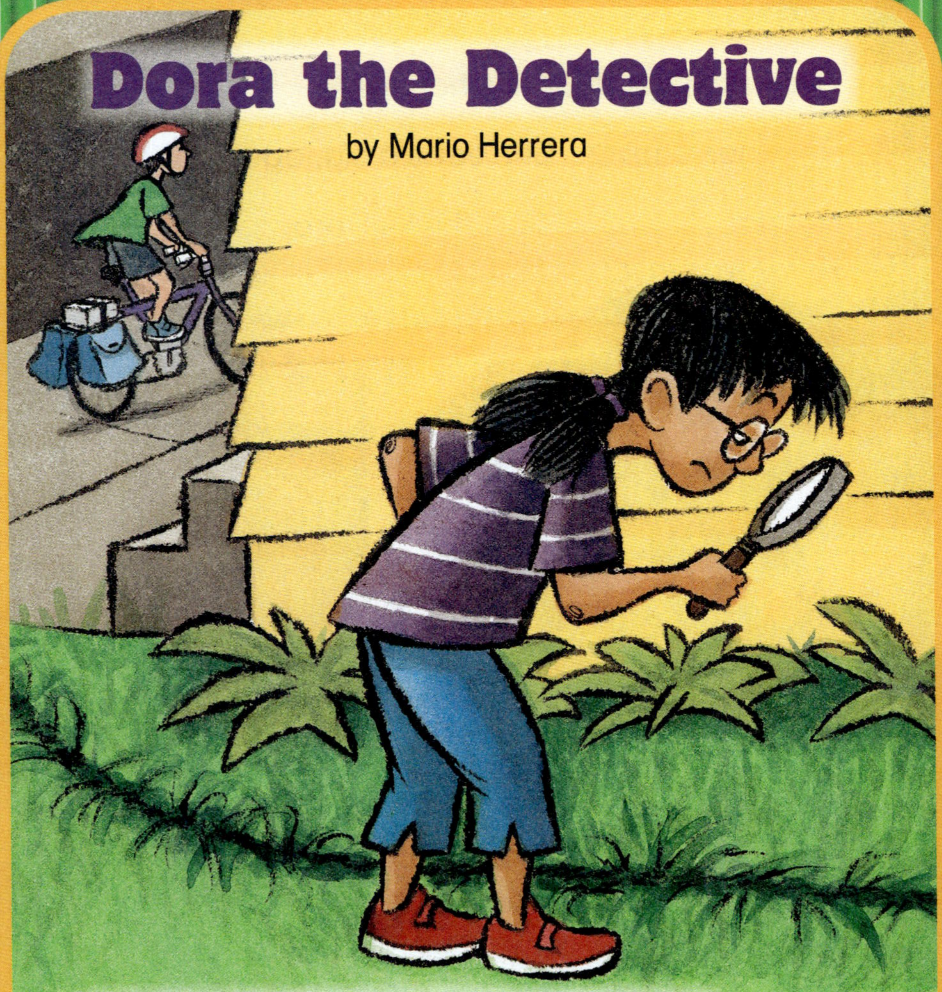

Dora likes to play detective.

What are these tracks? They look new, thinks Dora.

Dora follows the tracks.

TRACK A65

The tracks go to Dora's house.

Dora goes inside. She sees a big, open box.

Hmmm. An empty box, thinks Dora.
What was in it?

Dora goes into the kitchen.

Ugh! This cracker tastes bad, thinks Dora.

Dora hears a strange noise.

That sounds strange, thinks Dora.
What was it?

Accordian Book

Cut out the pictures on page 137.
Make and present a book about the five senses.

Content connection: science

Values

Share with Others

Look and read. Talk.

Share your new things.

Share your food.

Share your sports equipment.

What about you? When do you share? Talk and write.

____

____

____

Know It? Show It!

Draw six objects in six different squares. Take turns describing how an object looks, tastes, smells, feels, or sounds; and guessing the object.

B2.
It feels sticky.

Yes!
It's your turn.

Is it glue?

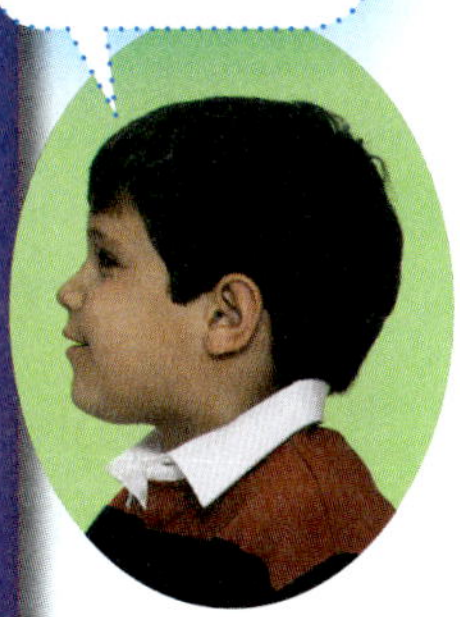

Take something from the grab bag. Describe how it feels, looks, sounds, tastes, or smells.

Unit 6
I can do it!

It's a yellow banana. Its skin feels smooth. It smells good and it tastes sweet.

Performance assessment
See Assessment Package pp. 87–89, 97, 106, 110–111, and 114–115.

7 A World of Food

TRACK B1

1 Read. Listen and sing.

Food, Glorious Food

In the morning, in the afternoon,
eating food is great.
Breakfast, lunch, or dinner—
I can hardly wait.
What do you have on your plate?

For breakfast I'll have
some toast and jam,
some milk and cereal,
some bread and ham.

At lunch time, I'm going to have
some soup,
a healthful salad,
and then some fruit.

(Chorus)

For dinner, I'll have
some fish and rice.
And for dessert,
perhaps cake would be nice.

Or maybe I'll have
onions and peas,
chicken and vegetables,
lettuce and cheese.

(Chorus)

TRACK B2

2 Listen. Point and say.

1. There is a loaf of bread on the table.
2. There are two pieces of cheese.
3. There is a jar of pickles.
4. There is a bunch of grapes.
5. There are three cans of soda.
6. There is a bottle of oil.
7. There are four slices of tomato.
8. There is a bowl of olives.

3 Stick and say.

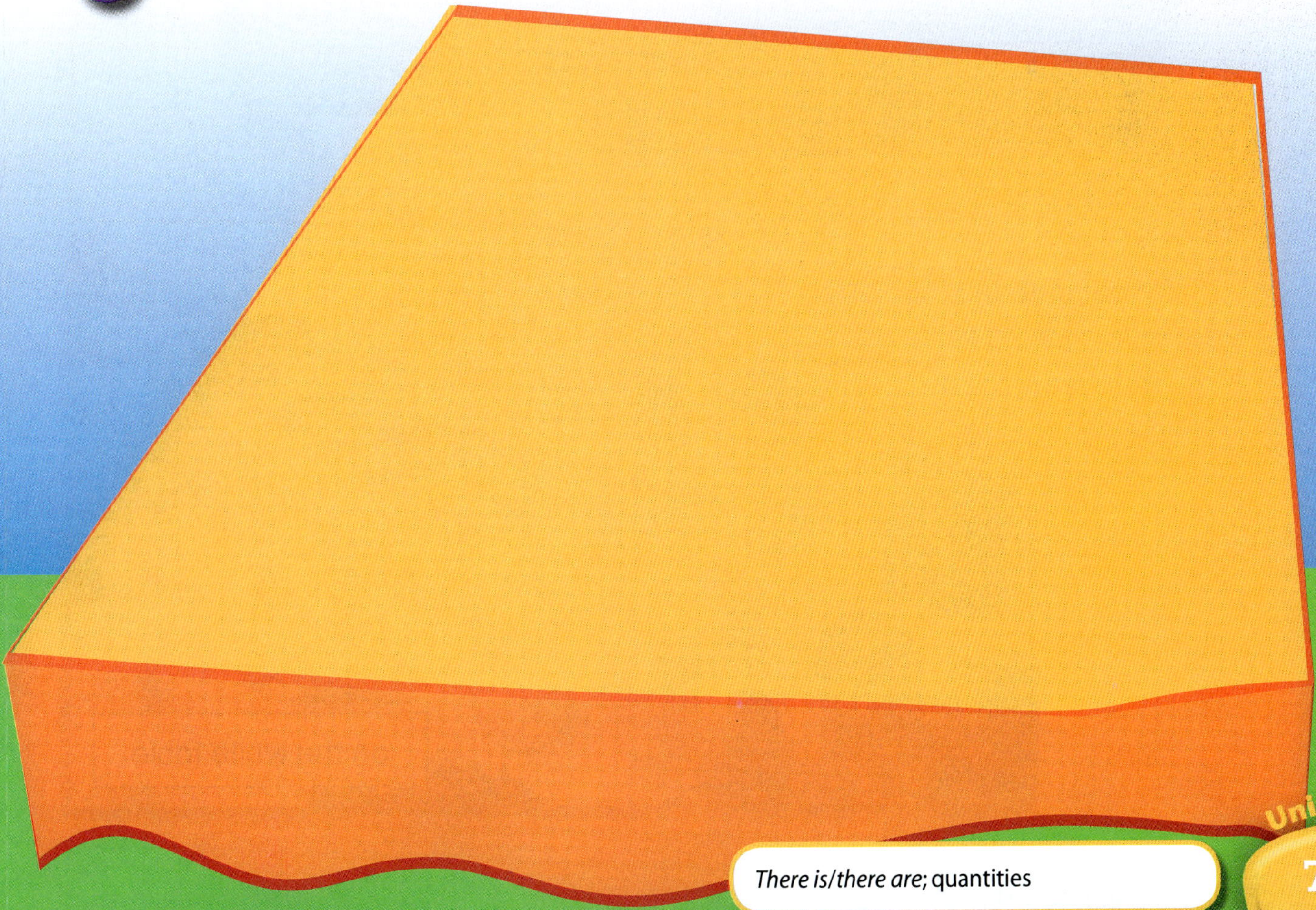

There is/there are; quantities

TRACK B4

4 Listen. Look and read.

The food we enjoy comes from all over the world.

Central and South America

Delicious bananas, mangoes, and pineapples come from Central and South America. So do vegetables such as peppers, corn, potatoes, asparagus, and tomatoes. Coffee and cocoa beans come from here, too.

in the basket

Asia

We get rice, tea, spinach, black pepper, pears, peaches, peas, onions, eggplants, and carrots from Asia.

on the white table

Europe

Foods such as broccoli, celery, cherries, garlic, and olives come from this part of the world. Many countries in this part of the world raise animals and sell a lot of beef, lamb, pork, chicken, and fish.

on the brown table

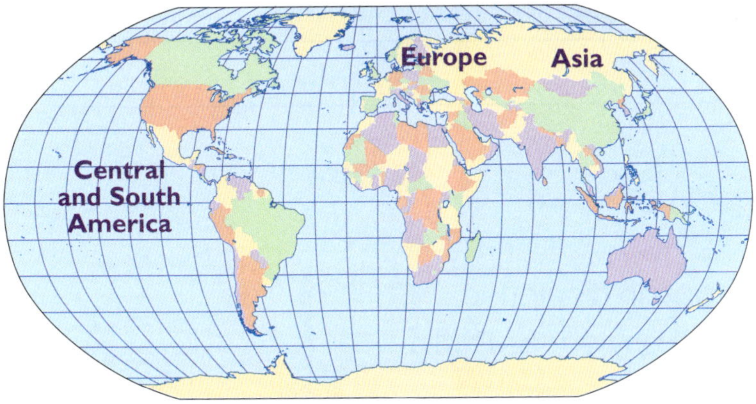

When you look at your dinner tonight, think about all the different places your food comes from!

5 Point. Ask and answer.

TRACK B5

What's on the brown table?

There is a plate of fish.

6 Ask and answer.

TRACK B6

Are there any cherries on the white table?

No. There aren't any.

Question formation; information and *yes/no* questions; quantities

Grammar

Are there any bananas in the basket? Yes, **there are** two bunches of bananas.
Are there any pears in the basket? No, **there aren't** any.

7 Look and write.

1. Are there any carrots? Yes, there are two bunches of carrots.
2. Are there any potatoes? ______
3. Are there any onions? ______
4. Are there any bananas? ______
5. Are there any cans of soda? ______
6. Are there any olives? ______

8 Read and write.

My friend Billy doesn't like the food in his house. There isn't any ice cream. There isn't any soda. There isn't any candy. There aren't any chips or salsa. Billy's mother doesn't want him to eat junk food. In Billy's kitchen, there are some carrots, some celery, some crackers, and some cheese. But no sweets!

1. Does Billy like the food in his house?

______

2. List four foods that aren't in Billy's house.

______

3. List four foods that are in Billy's house.

______

Yes/no questions; *there are/aren't*; quantifiers

9 What's in the refrigerator? Look and write.

1. There's a jar of pickles.
2. ______________________
3. ______________________
4. ______________________
5. ______________________
6. ______________________

What's your favorite breakfast?

10 Ask two friends. Tell the class.

Name	Breakfast	Lunch	Dinner
Charlie	apple juice toast and jam an egg	tomato soup cheese sandwich a banana	salad fish and rice ice cream
1.			
2.			

TRACK B8

11 Listen. Write T for *true* and F for *false*.

1. ____
2. ____
3. ____
4. ____
5. ____

1

2

3

4

5

TRACK B9

12 Listen. Read and chant.

Desserts

Pour some chocolate syrup
on top of your ice cream.
Put on a bright red cherry.
This dessert's a dream!

Take two chocolate cookies.
Put peanut butter on one.
Put the other cookie on top.
Cookie sandwiches are fun!

Ice cream, pie, and cookies.
I love a good dessert.
But never eat them all at once,
or your tummy will really hurt!

See Sound and Spelling Handbook p. 116

Listening for main idea and details; stress, rhythm, and intonation

Delicious Snacks

1. Put some pieces of fruit in a bowl.
2. Put in some orange juice and sugar.
3. Stir the fruit, orange juice, and sugar.
4. Put some coconut on top.
5. Eat and enjoy!

TRACK B10

1. Put pieces of banana and apple on a plate.
2. Dip each piece of fruit in honey.
3. Roll each piece in the crushed nuts.
4. Put in a toothpick.
5. Eat and enjoy!

1. Wash celery stalks and take off the leaves.
2. Cut each celery stalk into three pieces.
3. Put on some cream cheese.
4. Put raisins on top.
5. Eat and enjoy!

1. Put crackers on a plate.
2. Cut the guava paste and cheese into slices.
3. Put the pieces of cheese on the crackers.
4. Put a slice of guava paste on top.
5. Eat and enjoy!

Food Chart

Science Project

Complete the chart.

Food	What color?	How does it feel?	How does it smell?	How does it taste?
pineapple	brown, yellow	rough, sharp	sweet	sweet

Content connection: science; health

Help at Home

Look and read. Talk.

How do you help at home? Talk and write.

Know It? Show It!

Draw. Ask and answer.
How many foods are the same?
How many are different?

No, there aren't any apples.

Are there any apples in your drawing?

Make a favorite foods map.

Chocolate is one of my favorite foods. It comes from Mexico. Chocolate tastes sweet.

Performance assessment
See Assessment Package pp. 87–89, 98, 107, and 110–111.

8 In Shape!

TRACK B11

1 Read. Listen and sing.

Feeling Good

I eat lots of fruit and vegetables,
but not much pie or cake.
I drink lots of water and some juice
to keep me feeling great.

Outside, I get plenty of exercise.
I skate and ride my bike.
I play some soccer with my friends,
and sometimes, I take a hike.

I make sure when I'm at home
to look and feel my best.
I take a shower, brush my teeth,
and then get lots of rest.

'Cause I'm in shape and feeling good.
I know the rules for health.
Do like me, and you will learn
to take care of yourself!

(Chorus)

TRACK B12

2 Listen. Point and say.

Get in shape!

Get enough sleep.
Don't stay up too late.

Eat enough good food.
Don't eat too much junk food.

Get enough exercise.
Don't watch too much TV.

3 Stick and say.

TRACK B14

4 Listen. Look and read.

When you are in shape, you feel good. When you are out of shape, you don't feel good. How do you feel?

Today Taro feels good.

Yesterday Taro got plenty of sleep. He didn't stay up late. He ate plenty of fresh fruit and vegetables. He drank milk, juice, and water. Taro got plenty of exercise. It was a great day.

Today Teddy doesn't feel very good.

Yesterday Teddy didn't get enough sleep. Teddy didn't get enough exercise. He was in front of the TV all day. He didn't play soccer or go for a walk in the park.

Yesterday he ate too much junk food. He ate lots of candy, cookies, and potato chips. He drank a lot of soda. He didn't eat any fruit or vegetables.

TRACK B15

5 Point. Ask and answer.

TRACK B16

6 Point. Ask and answer.

Question formation with *yes/no* questions and information questions; simple past

Grammar

Did	you he she they	**get** enough sleep yesterday?	Yes,	I he she they	**did**.	No,	I he she they	**didn't**.

didn't = did not

7 Look and write.

1. Did she get enough sleep? ______________________
2. Did he drink enough water? ______________________
3. Did they get enough exercise? ______________________
4. Did he eat enough vegetables? ______________________

8 Read and write.

Yesterday Gina got plenty of sleep. She drank lots of water and juice. She ate plenty of fresh fruit and vegetables. She got lots of exercise on her bike. Her friend Tina didn't get enough sleep. She drank lots of soda. She ate too many chips and cookies. She didn't get any exercise.

1. Who's in shape? Why?

____

____

2. Who isn't in shape? Why?

____

____

Yes/no questions in simple past;
short answers in simple past

9 Ask three friends. Tell the class.

✔ = Yes, I did.
✘ = No, I didn't.

Name				
Mark	✘	✘	✔	✘
1.				
2.				
3.				

10 How do you get enough exercise? Check the boxes. Talk with a partner.

Yes/no questions and short answers in simple past; simple present

TRACK B18

11 Listen. Write the number.

TRACK B19

12 Listen. Read and chant.

Outside

I get together with my friends
to swim or fly our kites.
Sometimes we play basketball
or have races on our bikes.

We take some fruit and water
for a picnic in the park.
We climb and run and have great fun
until it's almost dark.

I just don't understand the kids
who stay inside all day.
Who cares about TV when you
can go outside to play?

See Sound and Spelling Handbook p. 117

Listening for details; stress, rhythm, and intonation

Jumping and riding help with balance.

Anita is jumping on a trampoline.
Justin is riding a horse.
They're having fun!

Exercise Is Fun!

How do children get enough exercise?

Climbing and dancing build strong muscles.

Boris is climbing a rock wall.
Asma is practicing ballet.
They're having fun!

TRACK B20

Gymnastics and karate
increase strength.

Barbara is doing gymnastics.
David is practicing karate.
They're having fun!

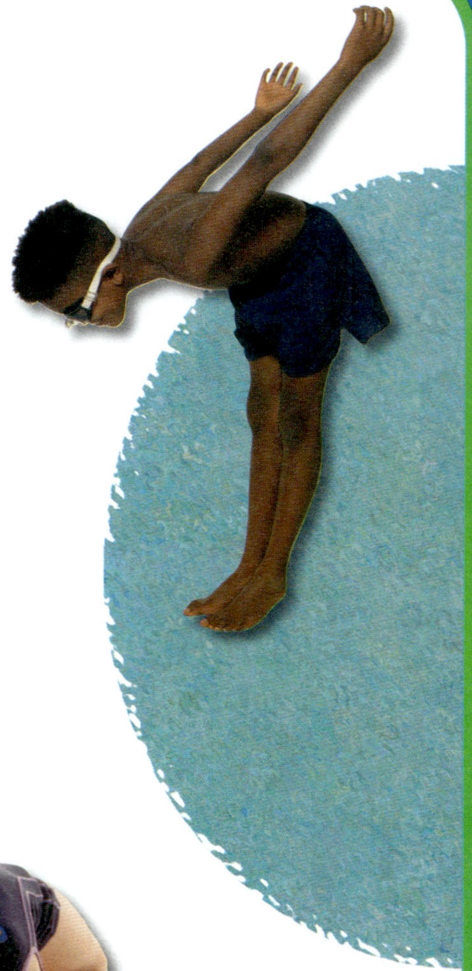

Diving and yoga
increase control.

Kenji is practicing diving.
Flor is doing yoga.
They're having fun!

My Progress Chart

Health Project

Choose health goals for yourself.
Make your own chart.

Did you eat more vegetables?

Yes, I did. Look. I ate green beans and carrots for lunch.

Content connection: health

Values

Get Exercise!

Look and read. Talk.

Play tag after school. It's fun and good exercise.

Dance to music! Dancing is fun and good exercise.

Walk your dog. It's good exercise for you and your pet!

How do you get exercise? Talk and write.

Know It? Show It!

Cut out the cards on page 139.
Talk about health rules.

Talk about a physical activity you enjoy.

Performance assessment
See Assessment Package pp. 87–89, 99, 108, and 110–111.

9 Puppets

TRACK B21

1 Read. Listen and sing.

Puppets for Sale

Do you want someone to play with?
Do you have an idea for a show?
I'm a puppet, and I'll be your friend.
I'm ready to play—let's go!

You can make a puppet, any size,
with paper bags, sticks, and things.
From a simple sock with a pair of eyes,
to a marionette with strings.

Some are thumb and finger puppets.
You can wear them on your hand.
Shadow puppets need a bright light
to do their shadow dance.

Do you want to tell a story
in a new, exciting way?
We are puppets, and we'll be your friends.
We're ready to go—let's play!

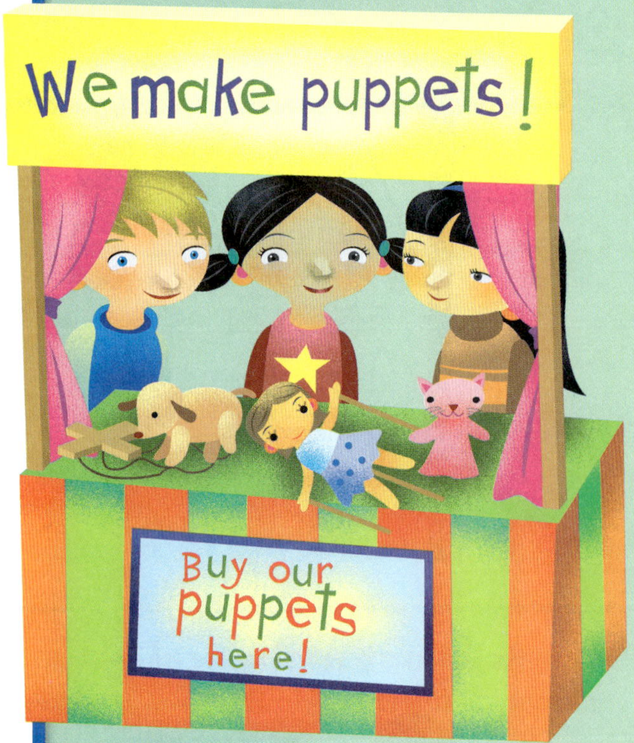

TRACK B22

2 Listen. Point and say.

1. I like puppets because they're funny.
2. I like puppets because they're exciting.
3. I like puppets because they're scary.
4. I don't like puppets because they're boring.

3 Stick and say.

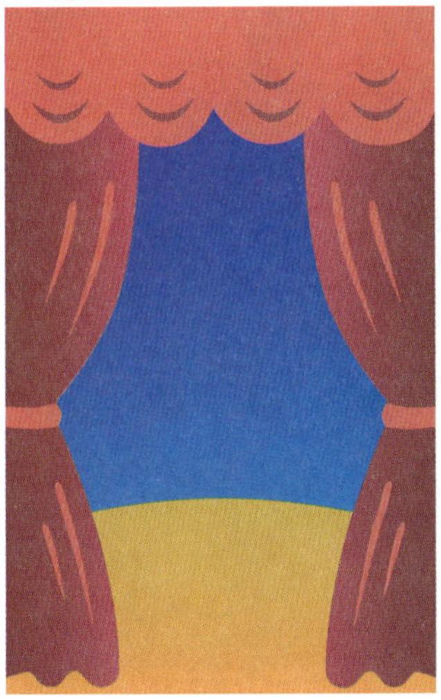

scary

boring

funny

exciting

TRACK B24

4 Listen. Look and read.

Puppets are popular all over the world.
Puppets can make us laugh or cry.
They can teach us history or tell us stories.

Check out these posters from the International Puppet Festival!

Flim, Flam, and Flopsy

Today at 3:00 P.M.

Flim and Flam can't find the queen's cat, Flopsy. You'll laugh at the funny things they do to catch Flopsy and take her back to the queen in her castle.

Stories from History: The Middle Ages

****

See history come to life with the famous

SICILIAN PUPPETS

Charlemagne	2:00 P.M.
Orlando Furioso	4:00 P.M.

TODAY

Reading: social studies; vocabulary and grammar in context

5 Point. Ask and answer.

TRACK B25

6 Ask and answer.

TRACK B26

Question formation with information and *yes/no* questions; simple past

Grammar

What **did**	you he she they	**see**?	I He She They	**saw** "Flim, Flam, and Flopsy."	

Did	you he she they	**like** it?	Yes,	I he she they	**liked** it a lot.	No,	I he she they	**didn't like** it.

7 Look and write.

1. What did they see?

____

2. Did he like it?

____

3. Did she like it?

____

Ghost Story

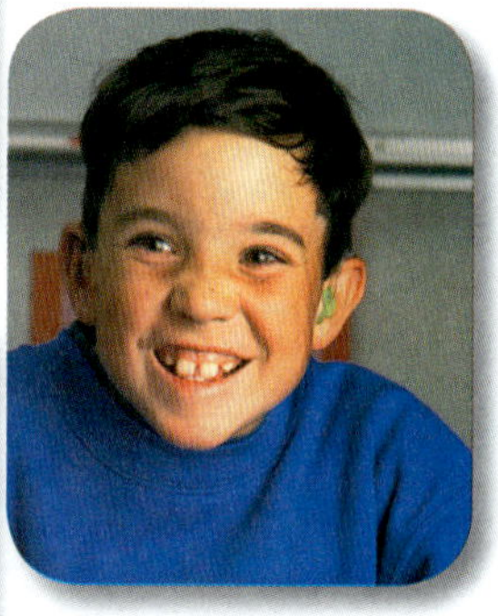

8 Read and write.

And now for my review of the "Punch & Judy" puppet show. The puppets in this show were very old, traditional puppets from Italy. They were colorful. The story was very funny. I laughed a lot. I think everyone will like this show. Take the family to see "Punch & Judy". I really liked it!

1. What did she see?

____

2. Did she like it? Why?

____

Question formation with information and *yes/no* questions; simple past

What do you like?
Why?

9 Ask two friends. Tell the class.

puppets

cartoons

movies

video games

sports

Name	What do you like?	Why?
Adrian	puppets and cartoons video games	because they are funny because they are exciting
1.		
2.		

10 Draw things you like. Write.

I like ____________________

because ____________________.

I like ____________________

because ____________________.

Information questions; simple present;
why/because

TRACK B28

11 Listen. Write the letter.

1. ____
2. ____
3. ____
4. ____
5. ____

a

b

c

d

e

TRACK B29

12 Listen. Read and chant.

Puppet Play

When you play with puppets,
  you're the puppeteer.
You decide what they will do—
  run or clap or cheer.

You can make their costumes,
  and decide what they will say.
Use your hand or strings to make
  them move a certain way.

You can paint their faces,
  and make them laugh or cry.
You can have them fight with swords
  or even throw a pie!

Your puppets are your actors
  to use in your own play.
With your own imagination,
  you'll have fun all day!

See Sound and Spelling Handbook p. 118

Listening for details; stress, rhythm, and intonation

Water Puppets

Water puppets look like they are walking or standing on water. The puppeteers stand in the water behind a screen and use long sticks to move the puppets.

Puppets Around the World

Marionettes

Marionettes are puppets with strings. Puppeteers use the strings to make the puppets move their heads, arms, and legs.

TRACK B30

Shadow Puppets

Shadow puppets have light behind them and a screen in front of them. They make shadows on the screen for people to see.

Rod Puppets

Rod puppets don't have strings. The puppeteers use sticks of wood or metal to move the puppets' heads, arms, and legs.

Puppet Play

Cut out the pictures on page 141. Make puppets and put on a play.

finger puppets

stick puppets

sock puppets

bag puppets

Content connection: art

Take Turns

Look and read. Talk.

When do you take turns? Talk and write.

Know It? Show It!

Move your marker. Listen and answer the question.

Talk about what you like and don't like.

Performance assessment
See Assessment Package pp. 87–89, 100, 109, 110–111, and 116–117.

Sound and Spelling Handbook

u as in *ruler*

TRACK B31

1 **Listen and say.**

TRACK B32

2 **Listen and say. Point to the picture.**

1
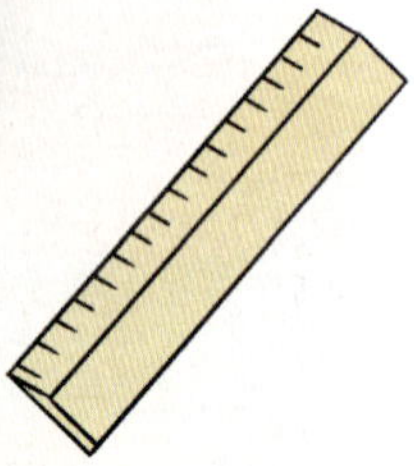

2

3

4

TRACK B33

3 **Listen. Which words have the same sound as the *u* in *ruler*? Circle the numbers.**

1 2 3 4 5

4 **Read. Underline the words with the same sound as the *u* in *ruler*.**

In January, we usually eat cake for dessert. But in June and July, we can eat lots of delicious fruit for dessert.

5 **Write words that have the same sound as the *u* in *ruler*.**

The colors yellow and ____________________ together make green.

My uncle Bob is a ____________________. He plays the trumpet.

TRACK B34

1 Listen and say.

TRACK B35

2 Listen and say. Point to the picture.

1 

2 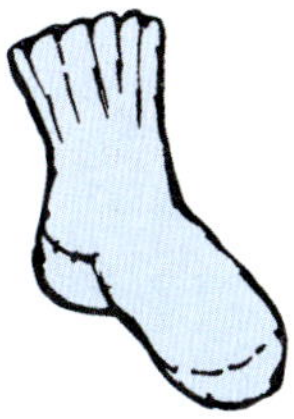

3 

4 

TRACK B36

3 Listen. Which words have the same sound as the **o** in *dog*? Check the boxes.

☐ ☐ ☐ ☐ ☐

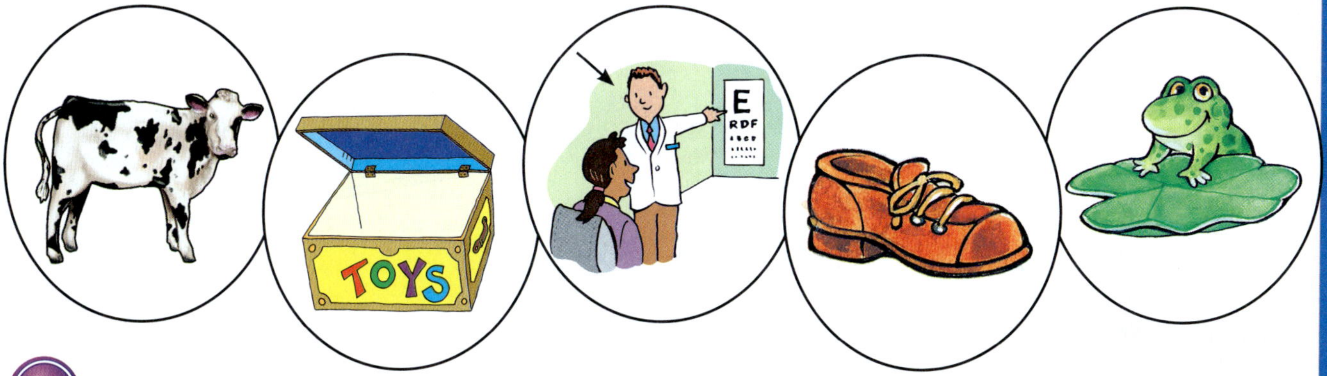

4 Read. Underline the words with the same sound as the **o** in *dog*.

I like animals a lot. I have a dog named Spot and a frog named Hoppy. And the bird on top of my head is Poppy!

5 Write words that have the same sound as the **o** in *dog*. Say.

You wear this on your foot, inside your shoe: ________________

You put your toys in this: ________________

You go to this person when you are sick: ________________

TRACK B37

1 Listen and say.

TRACK B38

2 Listen and say. Point to the picture.

1

2

3

4

TRACK B39

3 Listen. Which words have the same sound as the ***w*** in ***w*orm**? Trace the shapes.

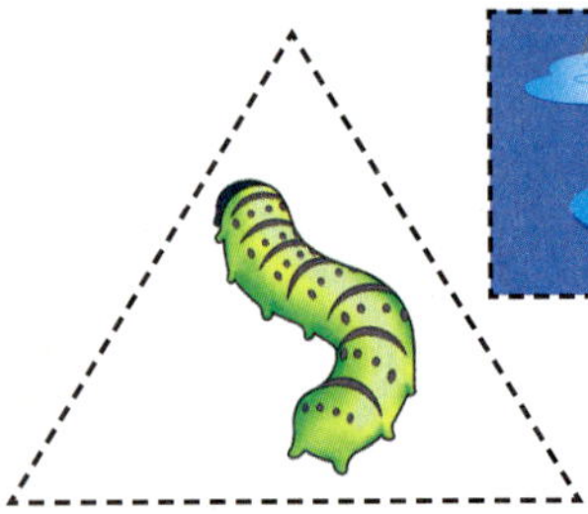

4 Read. Underline the words with the same sound as the ***w*** in ***w*orm.**

On Wednesday, we wash all our windows with soap and water. After our hard work, we rest and watch TV.

5 Look at 2. Write words that have the same sound as the ***w*** in ***w*orm.** Say.

________________ ________________

________________ ________________

TRACK B40

1 Listen and say.

TRACK B41

2 Listen and say. Point to the picture.

1  **2** 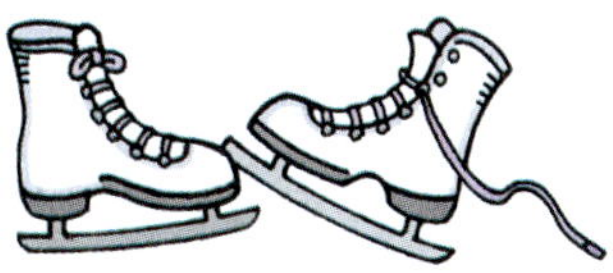 **3**  **4** 

TRACK B42

3 Listen. Which words have the same sound as the ***a*** in ***cake***? Connect the pictures.

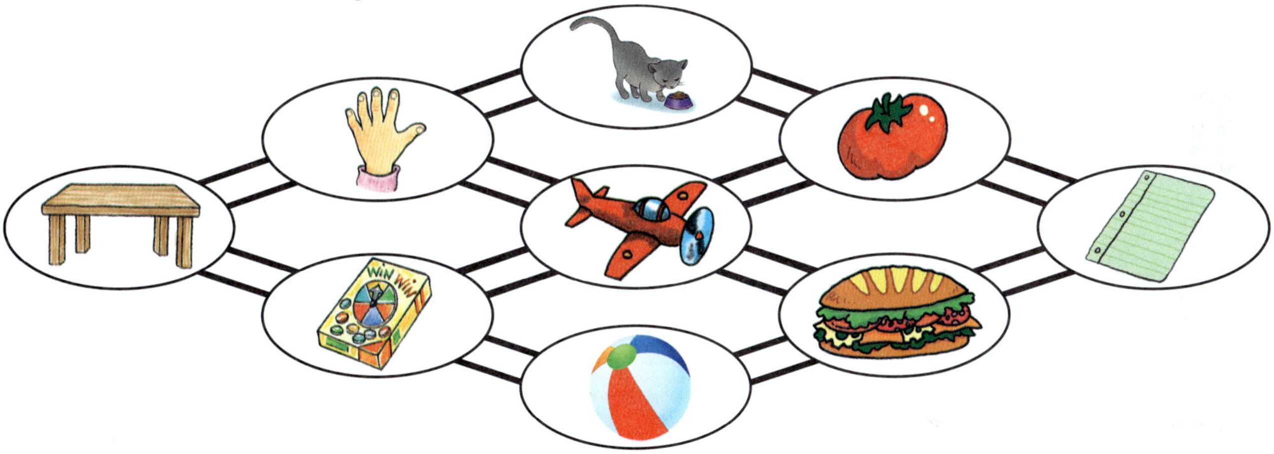

4 Read. Underline the words with the same sound as the ***a*** in ***cake***.

On Saturday, we go to my aunt Kay's house. She plays games with me, reads to me, and gives me cake and milk.

5 Look at 3. Write words that have the same sound as the ***a*** in ***cake***. Say.

____

____

TRACK B43

1 **Listen and say.**

TRACK B44

2 **Listen and say. Point to the picture.**

1

2

3

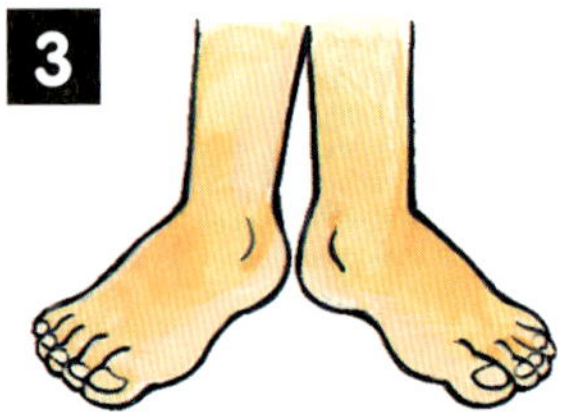

4

TRACK B45

3 **Listen. Which words have the same sound as the *e* in *zebra*? Color the blocks.**

4 **Read. Underline the words with the same sound as the *e* in *zebra*.**

I like to eat green beans, meat, and potatoes for dinner. Then I eat strawberry ice cream with a cookie for dessert.

5 **Write words that have the same sound as the *e* in *zebra*. Say.**

These are inside your mouth: ____________________

This number comes after twelve: ____________________

For a boy, say *he*; for a girl, say: ____________________

TRACK B46

1 Listen and say.

TRACK B47

2 Listen and say. Point to the picture.

1 

2 

3 

4 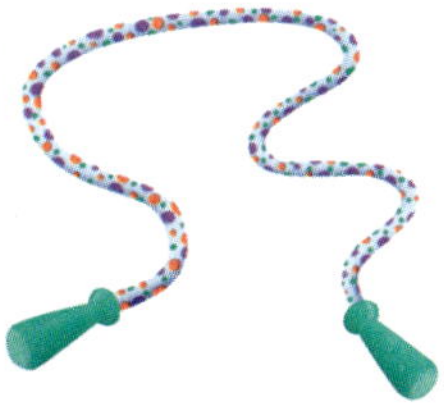

TRACK B48

3 Listen. Which words have the same sound as the *o* in *sofa*? Connect the pictures.

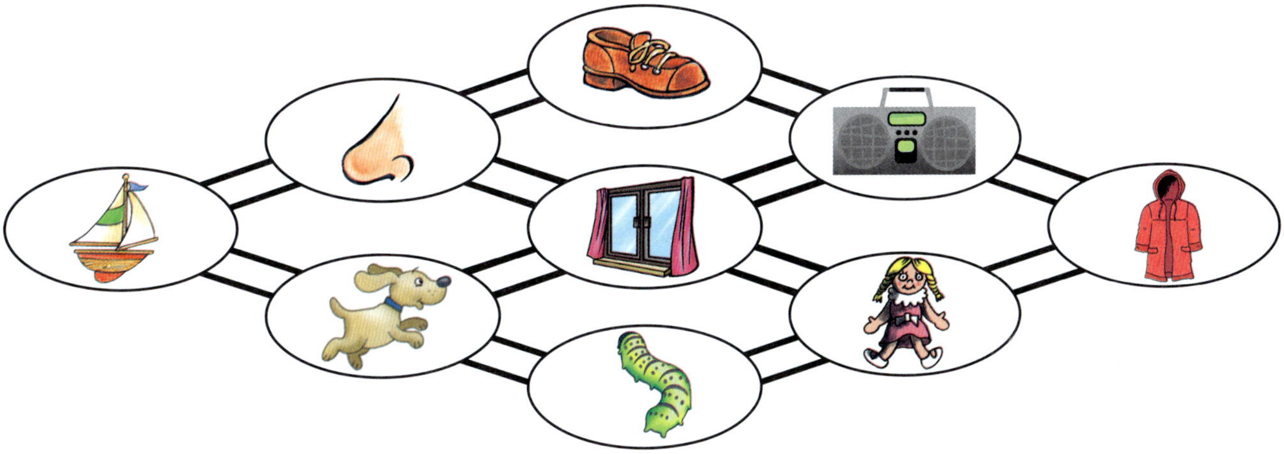

4 Read. Underline the words with the same sound as the *o* in *sofa*.

In November, I like to play outside in the snow for a long time. But then I get one red, runny nose and ten cold toes!

5 Write words that have the same sound as the *o* in *sofa*. Say.

A pretty red flower you can give your mother is a ______________________.

You can mail a letter at the ______________________.

In our kitchen there is a new ______________________.

TRACK B49

1 **Listen and say.**

TRACK B50

2 **Listen and say. Point to the picture.**

1

2

3

4
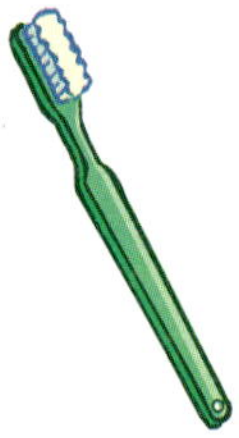

TRACK B51

3 **Listen. Which words have the same sound as the *sh* in *sh*oe? Check the boxes.**

☐ ☐ ☐ ☐ ☐

4 **Read. Underline the words with the same sound as the *sh* in *sh*oe.**

In the morning, I take a shower, brush my teeth, and get dressed in my favorite blue shirt, shorts, and shoes.

5 **Write words that have the same sound as the *sh* in *sh*oe. Say.**

Circles and triangles are ________________.

Polar bears have claws that are ________________.

TRACK B52

1 Listen and say.

TRACK B53

2 Listen and say. Point to the picture.

1

2

3

4

TRACK B54

3 Listen. Which words have the same sound as the *i* in *five*? Trace the shapes.

4 Read. Underline the words with the same sound as the *i* in *five.*

We are at the park. I'm riding my bike. My sister is playing hide-and-seek. My brother is flying his kite.

5 Write words that have the same sound as the *i* in *five*. Say the answer.

5 + 14 = ? ________________

20 + 70 = ? ________________

ch as in ***ch**air*

TRACK B55

1 Listen and say.

TRACK B56

2 Listen and say. Point to the picture.

1

2

3

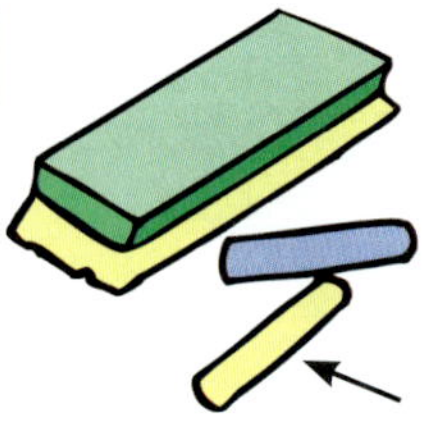

4

TRACK B57

3 Listen. Which words have the same sound as the *ch* in *ch*air? Check the stars.

4 Read. Underline the words with the same sound as the *ch* in *ch*air.

It's time for lunch. We have chicken sandwiches, salad, cheese pizza, and chocolate cake to eat. And juice to drink!

5 Write words that have the same sound as the *ch* in *ch*air. Say.

The t_______________ is writing with _______________ on the board. The _______________ are w_______________ her.

Review Units 1-3, Student A

Student A uses the information below.
Student B turns to page 120.

1. Number 1. What time does he do his homework?

   ____

3. Number 3. What do vets do?

   ____

5. Number 5. What does she sometimes do?

   ____

7. Number 7. What does she have to do?

   ____

9. Number 9. What does he do before breakfast?

   ____

2

4

6

8

10

Review Units 1-3, Student B

Student B uses the information below. Student A turns to page 119.

2. Number 2. What does she do after school?

   ____

4. Number 4. What time is it?

   ____

6. Number 6. What does your mother do?

   ____

8. Number 8. What does he always do?

   ____

10. Number 10. What do dentists do?

   ____

1

3

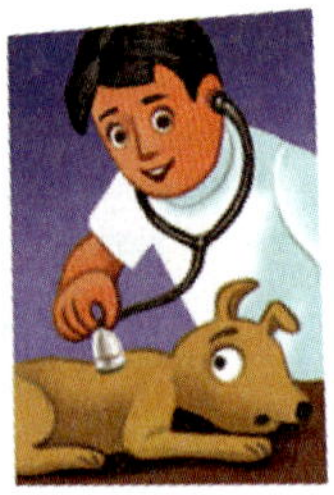

5

7

9

Review Units 4–6, Student A

Student A uses the information below. Student B turns to page 122.

1. Number 1. Where do penguins live?

____

3. Number 3. What does she wear in the spring?

____

5. Number 5. What's the weather like in summer?

____

7. Number 7. How does the music sound?

____

9. Number 9. Pick one thing. Describe it.

____

2

4

6

8

10

Review Units 4-6, Student B

Student B uses the information below. Student A turns to page 121.

2. Number 2. What can a camel do?

   ____

4. Number 4. What does he wear in the summer?

   ____

6. Number 6. What was the weather like yesterday?

   ____

8. Number 8. How do the children look?

   ____

10. Number 10. Pick one thing. Describe it.

   ____

1

3

5

7

9

Student A uses the information below. Student B turns to page 124.

1. Number 1. What's in the bowl?

 ____

3. Number 3. Did they get enough exercise?

 ____

5. Number 5. Are there any vegetables on the table?

 ____

7. Number 7. What did you see?

 ____

9. Number 9. What do you like? Why?

 ____

2

4

6

8

10

Student B uses the information below. Student A uses page 123.

2. Number 2. Is there any milk in the refrigerator?

____

4. Number 4. Did he get enough sleep last night?

____

6. Number 6. Did they eat enough vegetables for lunch?

____

8. Number 8. Did she like the movie? Why or why not?

____

10. Number 10. Are there any grapes?

____

1

3

5

7

9

Grammar and Writing

Writing is a process.

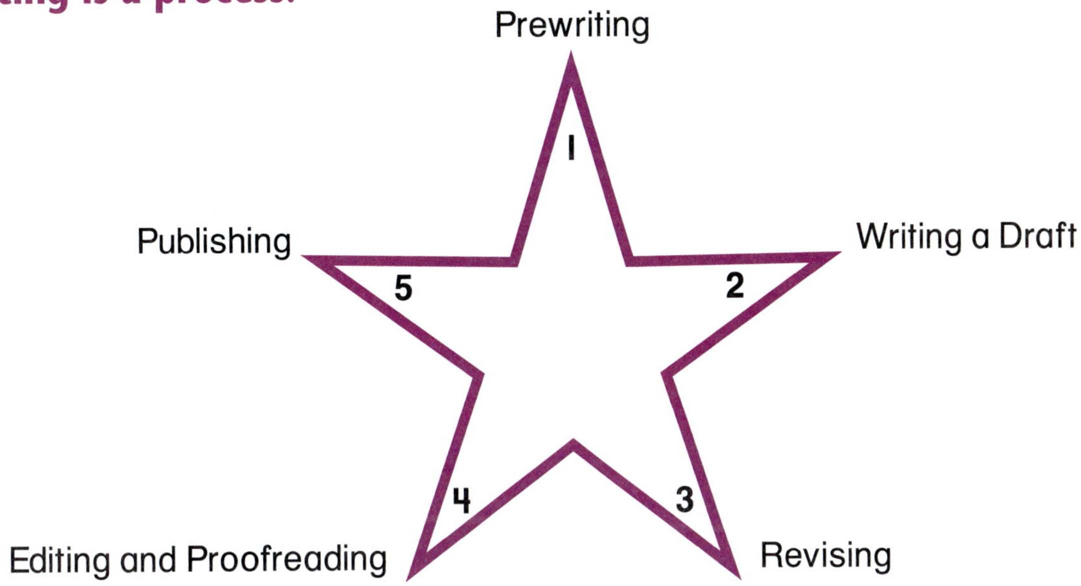

1. **Prewriting**
   a. Choose a topic.
   b. Collect information.
   c. Decide one main point to write about for your topic.

2. **Writing a Draft**
   a. Write all of your ideas on paper.
   b. Don't stop to check spelling or punctuation yet.

3. **Revising**
   a. Read your draft to yourself.
   b. Read your draft to a partner.
   c. Make changes to make your writing better.

4. **Editing and Proofreading**
   a. Make sure your writing makes sense.
   b. Check spelling, capitalization, and punctuation.
   c. Write a new, clean copy.

5. **Publishing**
   a. Share your writing with your teacher, classmates, and family.
   b. Post your writing on the classroom bulletin board or wall.
   c. Collect your best writing in a writing portfolio.

Parts of a Sentence

- ✔ A **sentence** is a group of words that tells a complete thought. We use sentences when we talk and when we write.

  Sandra watches TV after school.

- ✔ A sentence has different parts. The **subject** of a sentence tells *who* or *what* the sentence is about.

  Sandra watches TV after school.

- ✔ The **verb** of a sentence tells what the subject *is* or *does*.

  Sandra **watches** TV after school.

- ✔ The **predicate** of a sentence is the verb and the rest of the sentence.

  Sandra **watches TV after school.**

Simple Sentences

- ✔ A simple sentence has a subject and a verb.

  David runs.

- ✔ A simple sentence can have a **compound subject**, two subjects + *and* or *or*.

  David and Carlos run in the park.

- ✔ A simple sentence can have a **compound predicate**, two verbs + *and* or *or*.

  David **runs and swims** in the park.

- ✔ The **subject** and **verb** of a sentence must agree with one another.

  singular subject + singular verb: **Sandra watches** TV after school.
  plural subject + plural verb: **David and Carlos run** in the park.

Kinds of Sentences

Declarative sentences make a statement:	I have a new puppy.
Interrogative sentences ask a question:	Do you have a pet?
Imperative sentences give an order:	Put the collar on the puppy.
Exclamatory sentences show strong emotion:	Oh, no! He's running into the street!

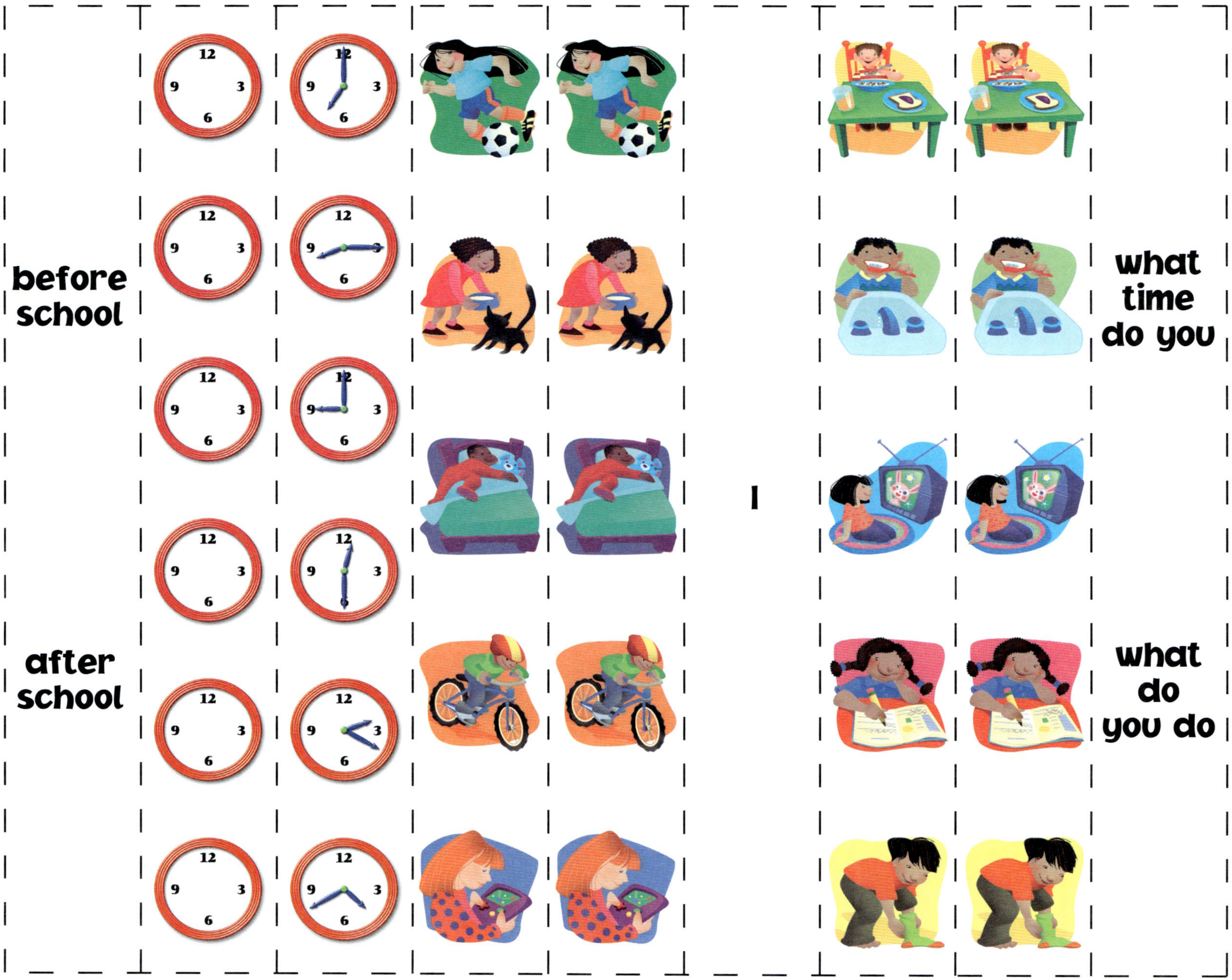
what time do you
what do you do
I
before school
after school

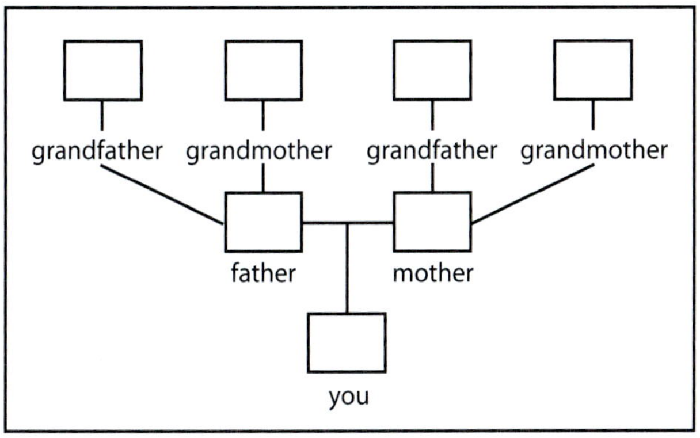
grandfather
grandmother
grandfather
grandmother
father
mother
you

CITY MUSEUM

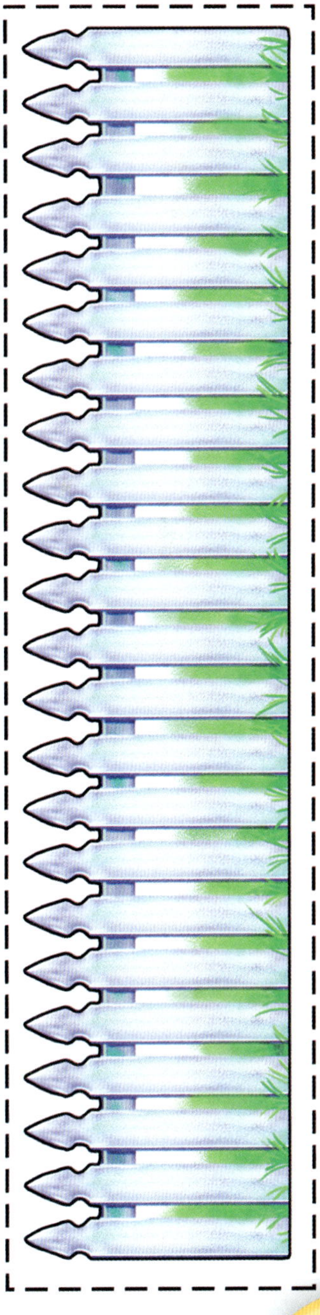

NOW
PLAYING

Animals from the plains

Animals from the ocean

Animals from the forest

Animals from cold places

PAINT

GLUE

CORN CHIPS
SALSA

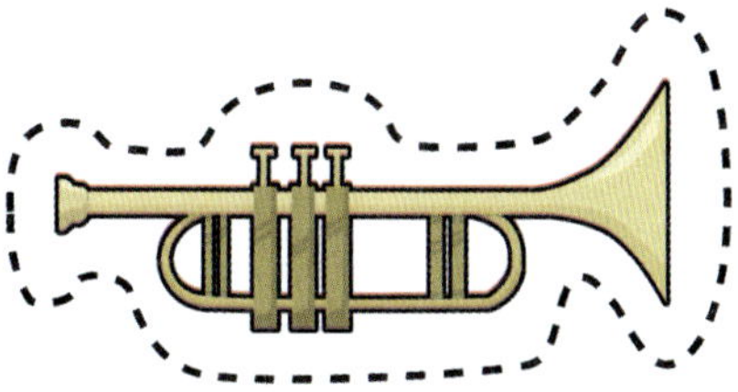

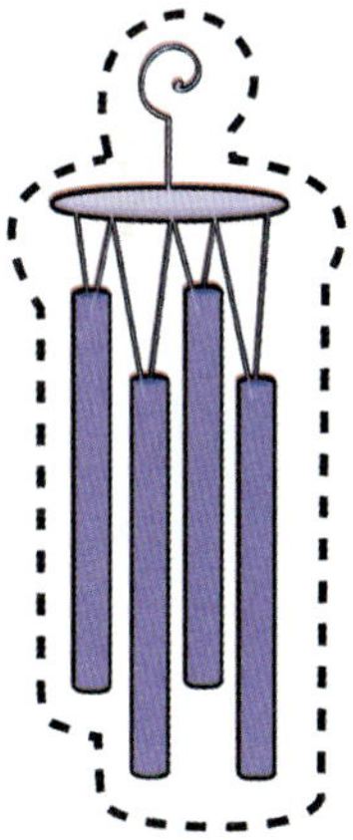

Stickers for Level 3

Unit 1

Unit 2

Unit 4

Unit 3

Unit 5

Unit 6

Unit 7

Unit 8

Unit 9

Completion Certificate Stickers

UNIT 1

UNIT 2

UNIT 3

UNIT 4

UNIT 5

UNIT 6

UNIT 7

UNIT 8

UNIT 9

BACKPACK 3 Certificate

____

has successfully completed Level 3.

______________________ ______________________

Teacher **Principal**